W9-CDO-283

At Issue

| World Hunger

Other books in the At Issue series:

At Issue

| World Hunger

Susan C. Hunnicutt, Book Editor

GREENHAVEN PRESS

An imprint of Thomson Gale, a part of The Thomson Corporation

Detroit • New York • San Francisco • New Haven, Conn. • Waterville, Maine • London

Christine Nasso, *Publisher*
Elizabeth Des Chenes, *Managing Editor*

© 2007 Thomson Gale, a part of The Thomson Corporation.

Thomson and Star logo are trademarks and Gale and Greenhaven Press are registered trademarks used herein under license.

For more information, contact:
Greenhaven Press
27500 Drake Rd.
Farmington Hills, MI 48331-3535
Or you can visit our Internet site at http://www.gale.com

LIBRARY OF CONGRESS CATALOGING-IN-PUBLICATION DATA

World hunger / Susan C. Hunnicutt, book editor.
    p. cm. -- (At Issue)
  Includes bibliographical references and index.
  ISBN-13: 978-0-7377-2761-6 (lib. : alk. paper)
  ISBN-10: 0-7377-2761-6 (lib. : alk. paper)
  ISBN-13: 978-0-7377-2762-3 (pbk. : alk. paper)
  ISBN-10: 0-7377-2762-4 (pbk. : alk. paper)
  1. Food supply--Juvenile literature. 2. Food relief--Juvenile literature. 3. Agriculture and state--Juvenile literature. 4. Genetic engineering--Juvenile literature.
  I. I. Hunnicutt, Susan.
  HD9000.5.W656 2007
  363.8--dc22

                                                        2006026204

Printed in the United States of America
10 9 8 7 6 5 4 3 2 1

Contents

Introduction

From the beginning of the 1960s to the end of the millennium, the population of the earth almost doubled, from 3 billion to 5.7 billion people, while the proportion of land devoted to growing crops grew by only 12 percent. This rapid increase in the number of people on the planet evoked the specter of a "population bomb." It set off fears of widespread starvation and food terrorism, and led to predictions of global famine and the development of a moral philosophy—lifeboat ethics—that was based on the idea that the earth would soon exceed what was termed its "carrying capacity."

The Green Revolution

By the 1990s, however, fears of imminent global famine had subsided. One reason for this was that the rate of population growth had slowed somewhat. But the most important factor lessening concern about a global food crisis was the Green Revolution, a series of innovations in plant breeding, chemical fertilizer and pesticide development, and irrigation technology that led to substantial increases in the planet's ability to produce food. Agricultural yields improved dramatically and crop disasters occurred less frequently. The result was that from 1962 to 1996, though the world's population increased by 90 percent, crop production worldwide increased 117 percent, far outstripping population growth. In some developing countries, including Thailand, Vietnam, and Brazil, the increase in agricultural productivity was as high as 175 percent. In the mid-1990s relief agencies began to contemplate the possibility that hunger could be completely eradicated.

That hope proved, however, to be overly optimistic: Today 842 million people worldwide, including 500 million children, are still undernourished. In 2004 the Food and Agriculture Organization of the United Nations (FAO) announced that the ranks of the hungry were once again increasing, by 5 million people per year, and that the goal of cutting the number of hungry people in half by 2015—set by the World Food Summit in 1996—would be unachievable. In 2005 the World Food Programme, a UN aid agency, announced that hunger was taking more lives than AIDS, malaria, and tuberculosis combined.

A Dramatic Change in Outlook

The paradox of rising malnutrition in the face of increased agricultural yields has prompted growing recognition that the problem of hunger is complex and multifaceted; solving it is no longer seen as a straightforward matter of producing more food, or even of producing enough food in the right locations. A broad range of location-specific economic and logistical factors mean that severe hunger often exists in the midst of agricultural abundance. For example, agricultural surpluses actually drive prices down so that the cost of producing food sometimes exceeds the profit that can be made by farmers. When this happens, rural poverty—and thus hunger—can increase even as food production swells. This situation exists in the United States as well as in many parts of the developing world.

Moreover, even where adequate quantities of food are obtainable, malnutrition can still be a problem if micronutrient deficiencies in the food supply prevent healthy growth and development. Micronutrients are trace elements such as vitamin A, iodine, iron, B vitamins, and folic acid. They are needed only in very small amounts, but they are vital: The lack of micronutrients can lead to birth defects such as spina bifida (caused by lack of folic acid) and to serious physical illnesses including blindness, mental handicaps, growth disorders, and impaired immune systems. The problem of hunger is thus not simply a matter of the amount of food consumed, but of its quality and variety as well.

No matter what form hunger takes, participants in the debate surrounding the problem of world hunger increasingly are calling attention to its myriad causes. These include political or civil strife, which has led to famine among refugee populations in the Sudan, Afghanistan, Pakistan, Guinea, and Sierra Leone. Natural disasters, such as the 2004 Asian tsunami and more recent earthquakes, also contribute to the problem. Despite the Green Revolution, hunger in many developing countries is a result of economic policies that discriminate against local agricultural initiatives. Farmers may not have access to locally appropriate technology, rural financial institutions may be inefficient, transportation infrastructure may be inadequate, and marketing services may be scarce. Women, who bear the bulk of the burden of providing food for families throughout the world, may lack access to needed education and resources or be subject to societal pressures and customs that limit their ability to participate fully in the economy. Climate change may also contribute to increases in world hunger, and trade policies most certainly do, although exactly how is a subject that is hotly debated.

This clearly complex and urgent problem has sparked numerous opinions about its causes and possible solutions. The contributors to *At Issue: World Hunger* provide a number of different contemporary perspectives on the reasons for world hunger. They also examine ways in which the problem may—or may not—finally be solved.

1

World Hunger Is a Worsening Problem

UN Chronicle

The UN Chronicle *is a publication of the Outreach Division of the United Nations Department of Public Information.*

After significant successes in fighting hunger in the early 1990s, the Food and Agriculture Organization of the United Nations reports an increase in levels of hunger worldwide in recent years. Lack of water is the most common cause of severe food shortages, but systemic poverty and limited opportunities for trade also play roles. Generally, the greatest successes in reducing hunger have occurred in countries that have also experienced increases in economic and agricultural productivity.

Hunger is on the rise again after falling steadily during the first half of the 1990s, states the Food and Agriculture Organization of the UN (FAO) in its annual report, *The State of Food Insecurity in the World 2003* (SOFI 2003). Its latest estimates signal a setback in the war against hunger.

Goals Cannot Be Reached

Given the rate at which hunger has declined since 1990 on average, the World Food Summit goal of reducing by half the undernourished people by 2015 cannot be reached. After falling by 37 million during the first half of the 1990s, the number of hungry people in developing countries increased by 18

UN Chronicle, "Setback in the War Against Hunger (Food Watch)," vol. 40, December 2003, p. 66. © 2003 United Nations. Reprinted with the permission of the United Nations.

million in the second half. According to Hartwig de Haen, Assistant Director-General in the FAO Economic and Social Department, "the goal can only be reached if the recent trend of increasing numbers is reversed. The annual reductions must be accelerated to 26 million per year, more than 12 times the pace of 2.1 million per year achieved during the 1990s."

FAO estimates that 842 million people worldwide were undernourished in 1999 to 2001, the most recent years for which figures are available. This includes 10 million in industrialized countries, 34 million in countries in transition and 798 million in developing countries. Regionally, only Latin America and the Caribbean had a decline in the number of hungry people since the mid-1990s. Only 19 countries, including China, succeeded in reducing the number of undernourished throughout the 1990s, the report says. "In these successful countries, the total number of hungry people fell by over 80 million."

FAO estimates that 842 million people worldwide were undernourished in 1999 to 2001.

At the other end of the scale are 26 countries where the undernourished increased by 60 million during the same period. Twenty-two countries, including Bangladesh, Haiti and Mozambique, succeeded in turning the tide against hunger. In these countries, the undernourished "declined during the second half of the decade after rising through the first five years," the report said. "In 17 other countries, however, the trend shifted in the opposite direction and the number of undernourished people, which had been falling, began to rise," including a number with large populations, among them India, Indonesia, Nigeria, Pakistan and the Sudan. Several countries in Central and West Africa have seen an increase due to conflict. In some successful countries, progress slowed after dramatic gains in the early 1990s. Having reduced chronic undernourishment to moderate or low levels, "these countries can no longer be expected to propel progress for the developing world," the report says. Countries in transition showed an overall increase of 9 million between the periods of 1993–1995 to 1999–2001.

Many Factors Impact Food Security

Preliminary analysis suggests that countries with significantly higher economic and agricultural growth had the most success in reducing hunger, the report states.

Other factors that contributed to success include lower population growth and higher levels of economic and social development. Those countries with a high prevalence of chronically hungry people are also afflicted by frequent food emergencies and high rates of HIV/AIDS. In fact, the southern African food crisis of 2002–2003 showed that "hunger cannot be combated effectively in regions ravaged by AIDS unless interventions address the particular needs of AIDS-affected households and incorporate measures both to prevent and to mitigate the spread of HIV/AIDS."

SOFI 2003 also looks at the impact of water on food security and hunger, calling drought "the single most common cause of severe food shortages in developing countries." Africa stands as a stark example of this, being the continent with the most prevalent hunger and the driest in the developing world. Achieving food security in countries where water is scarce and the environment is fragile may rely on what is known as "virtual water," through food imports. Says FAO: "It may make sense to import food and use limited water resources for other purposes, including growing high value crops for export."

Agriculture and agricultural trade in developing countries play a particularly important role in the national economies and food security of developing countries. "Countries where more than 15 per cent of the population goes hungry spend more than twice as much of their export earnings to import food as more food-secure countries," according to the report. "But their poverty and limited trading activities constrict both their export earnings and their ability to buy more food on international markets."

SOFI 2003 urges the wider adoption and support of the global Anti-Hunger Programme, proposed by FAO recently, which outlines a twin-track approach that advocates a combination of measures that increase the agricultural productivity in poorer rural communities with action to give hungry people immediate access to the food they need. The Programme sets out priorities and budgets for action in five areas: improving agricultural productivity in poor rural communities; developing and conserving natural resources; expanding rural infrastructure and market access; strengthening capacity for knowledge generation and dissemination; and ensuring access to food for the most needy.

"Ultimately," said Mr. de Haen, "success in reducing hunger will depend on mustering the political will to engage in policy reforms and invest resources where they can do the most good for the poor and hungry."

2

Increasing Crop Yields Will Reduce World Hunger

Mark W. Rosegrant and Sarah A. Cline

Mark W. Rosegrant and Sarah A. Cline are with the International Food Policy Research Institute.

Crop yields have fallen recently in many parts of the world. Reasons for decreased agricultural production include the declining levels of investment in research and infrastructure and the scarcity of water. Climate changes and epidemics such as HIV/AIDS are also factors impacting crop yields. Increased investments in agricultural research, education, water and transport infrastructure, and local solutions are among the policy measures that will increase crop yields and lead to greater global food security.

The ability of agriculture to support growing populations has been a concern for generations and continues to be high on the global policy agenda. The eradication of poverty and hunger was included as one of the United Nations Millennium Development Goals adopted in 2000. One of the targets of the Goals is to halve the proportion of people who suffer from hunger between 1990 and 2015. Meeting this food security goal will be a major challenge. Predictions of food security outcomes have been a part of the policy landscape since [English economist Thomas] Malthus' *An Essay on the Principle of Population* of 1798. Over the past several decades, some experts have expressed concern about the ability of agricultural production to keep up with global food demands, whereas others have forecast that technological advances or expansions of cultivated areas would boost production sufficiently to meet rising demands. So far, dire predictions of a global food security catastrophe have been unfounded.

Declining Crop Yields Are a Problem

Nevertheless, crop yield growth has slowed in much of the world because of declining investments in agricultural research, irrigation, and rural infrastructure and increasing water scarcity. New challenges to food security are posed by climate change and the morbidity and mortality of human immunodeficiency virus/acquired immunodeficiency syndrome (HIV/AIDS). Many studies predict that world food supply will not be adversely affected by moderate climate change, by assuming farmers will take adequate steps to adjust to climate change and that additional CO_2 [carbon dioxide] will increase yields. However, many developing countries are likely to fare badly. In warmer or tropical environments, climate change may result in more intense rainfall events between prolonged dry periods, as well as reduced or more variable water resources for irrigation. Such conditions may promote pests and disease on crops and livestock, as well as soil erosion and desertification. Increasing development into marginal lands may in turn put these areas at greater risk of environmental degradation. The HIV/AIDS epidemic is another global concern, with an estimated 42 million cases worldwide at the end of 2002, 95% of those are in developing countries. In addition to its direct health, economic, and social impacts, the disease also affects food security and nutrition. Adult labor is often removed from affected households, and these households will have less capacity to produce or buy food, as assets are often depleted for medical or funeral costs. The agricultural knowledge base will deteriorate as individuals with farming and science experience succumb to the disease. Can food security goals be met in the face of these old and new challenges?

Increased investment in people is essential to accelerate food security improvements.

Several organizations have developed quantitative models that project global food supply and demand into the future. According to the most recent baseline projections of the International Food Policy Research Institute's (IFPRI's) International Model for Policy Analysis of Agricultural Commodities and Trade (IMPACT), global cereal production is estimated to increase by 56% between 1997 and 2050, and livestock production by 90%. Developing countries will account for 93% of cereal-demand growth and 85% of meat-demand growth to 2050. Income growth and rapid urbanization are major forces driving increased demand for higher valued commodities, such as meats, fruits, and vegetables. International agricultural trade will increase substantially, with developing countries' cereal imports doubling by 2025 and tripling by 2050. Child malnutrition will persist in many developing countries, although overall, the share of malnourished children is projected to decline from 31% in 1997 to 14% in 2050. Nevertheless, this represents a nearly 35-year delay in meeting the Millennium Development Goals. In some places, circumstances will deteriorate, and in sub-Saharan Africa, the number of malnourished preschool children will increase between 1997 and 2015, after which they will only decrease slightly until 2050. South Asia is another region of concern—although progress is expected in this region, more than 30% of preschool children will remain malnourished by 2030, and 24% by 2050.

Reform Is Needed on Many Fronts

Achieving food security needs policy and investment reforms on multiple fronts, including human resources, agricultural research, rural infrastructure, water resources, and farm- and community-based agricultural and natural resources management. Progressive policy action must not only increase agricultural production, but also boost incomes and reduce poverty in rural areas where most of the poor live. If we take such an approach, we can expect production between 1997 and 2050 to increase by 71% for cereals and by 131% for meats. A reduction in childhood malnutrition would follow; the number of malnourished children would decline from 33 million in 1997 to 16 million in 2050 in sub-Saharan Africa, and from 85 million to 19 million in South Asia.

Much could be achieved by water conservation and increased efficiency in existing systems and by increased crop productivity per unit of water used.

Increased investment in people is essential to accelerate food security improvements. In agricultural areas, education works directly to enhance the ability of farmers to adopt more advanced technologies and crop-management techniques and to achieve higher rates of return on land. Moreover, education encourages movement into more remunerative nonfarm work, thus increasing household income. Women's education affects nearly every dimension of development, from lowering fertility rates to raising productivity and improving environmental management. Research in Brazil shows that 25% of children were stunted if their mothers had four or fewer years of schooling; however, this figure fell to 15% if the mothers had a primary education and to 3% if mothers had any secondary education. Poverty reduction is usually enhanced by an increase in the proportion of educational resources going to primary education and to the poorest groups or regions. Investments in health and nutrition, including safe drinking water, improved sewage disposal, immunization, and public health services, also contribute to poverty reduction. For example, a study in Ethiopia shows that the distance to a water source, as well as nutrition and morbidity, all affect agricultural productivity of households.

When rural infrastructure has deteriorated or is nonexistent, the cost of marketing farm produce, and thus escaping subsistence agriculture and improving incomes, can be prohibitive for poor farmers. Rural roads increase agricultural production by bringing new land into cultivation and by intensifying existing land use, as well as consolidating the links between agricultural and nonagricultural activities within rural areas and between rural and urban areas. Government expenditure on roads is the most important factor in poverty alleviation in rural areas of India and China, because it leads to new employment opportunities, higher wages, and increased productivity.

In addition to being a primary source of crop and livestock improvement, investment in agricultural research has high economic rates of return. Three major yield-enhancing strategies include research to increase the harvest index, plant biomass, and stress tolerance (particularly drought resistance). For example, the hybrid "New Rice for Africa," which was bred to grow in the uplands of West Africa, produces more than 50% more grain than current varieties when cultivated in traditional rainfed systems without fertilizer. Moreover, this variety matures 30 to 50 days earlier than current varieties and has enhanced disease and drought tolerance. In addition to conventional breeding, recent developments in nonconventional breeding, such as marker-assisted selection and cell and tissue culture techniques, could be employed for crops in developing countries, even if these countries stop short of transgenic breeding. To date, however, application of molecular biotechnology has been mostly limited to a small number of traits of interest to commercial farmers, mainly developed by a few global life science companies.

Although much of the science and many of the tools and intermediate products of biotechnology are transferable to solve high-priority problems in the tropics and subtropics, it is generally agreed that the private sector will not invest sufficiently to make the needed adaptations in these regions with limited market potential. Consequently, the public sector will have to play a key role, much of it by accessing proprietary tools and products from the private sector.

The Importance of Water

Irrigation is the largest water user worldwide, but also the first sector to lose out as scarcity increases. The challenges of water scarcity are heightened by the increasing costs of developing new water sources, soil degradation in irrigated areas, groundwater depletion, water pollution, and ecosystem degradation. Wasteful use of already developed water supplies may be encouraged by subsidies and distorted incentives that influence water use. Hence, investment is needed to develop new water management policies and infrastructure. Although the economic and environmental costs of irrigation make many investments unprofitable, much could be achieved by water conservation and increased efficiency in existing systems and by increased crop productivity per unit of water used. Regardless, more research and policy efforts need to be focused on rainfed agriculture. Exploiting the full potential of rainfed agriculture will require investment in water harvesting technologies, crop breeding, and extension services, as well as good access to markets, credit, and supplies. Water harvesting and conservation techniques are particularly promising for the semi-arid tropics of Asia and Africa, where agricultural growth has been less than 1% in recent years. For example, water harvesting trials in Burkina Faso, Kenya, Niger, Sudan, and Tanzania show increases in yield of a factor of 2 to 3, compared with dryland farming systems.

Agroecological approaches that seek to manage landscapes for both agricultural production and ecosystem services are another way of improving agricultural productivity. A study of 45 projects, using agroecological approaches, in 17 African countries shows cereal yield improvements of 50 to 100 percent. There are many concomitant benefits to such approaches, as they reduce pollution through alternative methods of nutrient and pest management, create biodiversity reserves, and enhance habitat quality through careful management of soil, water, and natural vegetation. Important issues remain about how to scale up agroecological approaches. Pilot programs are needed to work out how to mobilize private investment and to develop systems for payment of ecosystem services. All of these issues require investment in research, system development, and knowledge sharing.

Local Solutions Will Yield Results

To implement agricultural innovation, we need collective action at the local level, as well as the participation of government and nongovernmental organizations that work at the community level. There have been several successful programs, including those that use water harvesting and conservation techniques. Another priority is participatory plant breeding for yield increases in rainfed agrosystems, particularly in dry and remote areas. Farmer participation can be used in the very early stages of breed selection to help find crops suited to a multitude of environments and farmer preferences. It may be the only feasible route for crop breeding in remote regions, where a high level of crop diversity is required within the same farm, or for minor crops that are neglected by formal breeding programs.

Making substantial progress in improving food security will be difficult, and it does mean reform of currently accepted agricultural practices. However, innovations in agro-ecological approaches and crop breeding have brought some documented successes. Together with investment in research and water and transport infrastructure, we can make major improvements to global food security, especially for the rural poor.

3

Free-Trade Policies Can Reduce World Hunger

John Nash and Donald Mitchell

John Nash is the adviser for commodities and trade in the World Bank's Rural Development Department. Donald Mitchell is the lead economist in the bank's Development Prospects Group.

The earth produces more than enough food to feed everyone. In spite of this, more than 840 million people worldwide are undernourished. Part of the problem is the widespread belief that the key to fighting hunger is increasing crop production. Another issue is that many countries impose protectionist trade barriers (tariffs) in order to support the income of their own farmers. A better approach would improve access to food worldwide by removing trade barriers and improving transportation infrastructure; this approach would improve the purchasing power of poor people by raising incomes and strengthening local economies.

Trade policy may not, at first glance, seem like the ideal tool for combating hunger. But eradicating costly protectionist barriers may be one of the best ways to put food on the tables of the poor. The world produces more than enough food to feed everyone. Yet about 840 million people, or almost one-sixth of the world's population, still suffer from undernourishment. The overwhelming majority of these—about 92 percent—suffer from chronic undernutrition, rather than the acute hunger that grabs headlines in periods of man-made or natural disasters.

Increased Production Is Not the Answer

Part of the problem is the obsession in both developed and developing countries with the idea that increasing national food crop production, rather than raising incomes, is the best way to achieve food security. This preoccupation in developing countries has been exacerbated by the inordinately high support for agricultural production in industrialized countries, which causes huge distortions in global food markets. It has been a costly distraction both in countries' own policies and in negotiations in the World Trade Organization's (WTO) Doha Round trade talks.

Global trade liberalization is only one weapon in the arsenal to fight hunger, but it can make an important contribution by delivering cheaper food in protectionist countries and boosting the global economy, helping to lift millions out of poverty. This is one reason why it is essential that the Doha Round agreement lower barriers to trade in food products in rich and poor countries. This [viewpoint] examines how trade policy can be harnessed to help reduce poverty and alleviate hunger and outlines an agenda to reduce food insecurity in developing countries.

Food production, stocks, and exporting capacity are not at the root of the problem of undernutrition. Grain prices have been falling over the past 25 years thanks to global surpluses. Despite a reduction in global cropland used for grain production, particularly in the five largest exporting areas—the United States, the European Union (EU), Canada, Australia, and Argentina—real prices for wheat have fallen by about 34 percent and for rice by almost 60 percent. The 2004/05 crop year is expected to see world grain production increase by 8 percent, the biggest year-on-year increase in 26 years, as a result of higher yields and better growing conditions in regions plagued by several years of drought. With consumption projected to increase by only 2 percent, the boost in production should lead to higher grain stocks.

Protectionist Trade Policies Are Not the Answer

In spite of adequate global supplies, and in part thanks to relatively low world prices, many countries impose import tariffs on food to encourage and protect higher-cost domestic production. While this is true of both industrialized and developing countries, the latter bear the brunt of much of the cost of both their own protectionist policies and those of the richer countries. Food protectionism results in higher domestic food prices, which mostly hurt poor consumers as they spend disproportionately on food. Protectionism does not benefit the rural poor equally as it leaves out two large groups: those who do not own farmland, but have to pay higher prices as consumers; and those who own farmland, but do not produce for commercial purposes. And even commercial farmers, who may see a short-term increase in their income, will not experience long-term benefits such as a significant narrowing of the income gap with nonfarmers; this will come only from measures that raise agricultural productivity and facilitate the movement of labor.

Policymakers often view protectionism as a substitute for more productive methods in support of agriculture, such as increased spending on rural education, infrastructure, research, and technical assistance. It keeps them from investing in efficient food distribution systems that would improve their ability to respond quickly to food emergencies. Simulations have shown that replacing the implicit tax on consumption that results from protectionism with an equivalent explicit tax and investing the revenue in agricultural research can be enormously beneficial for increasing employment, income, and consumption, particularly of food.

Protectionism also indirectly encourages farmers to continue planting low-value food crops instead of diversifying into high-value nontraditional exports that would be a better way of raising income and escaping poverty. In turn, the lack of export production reduces the country's ability to earn foreign exchange and undermines its structural capacity to import food and other products. And when many developing countries protect their food crops by imposing import tariffs, they are effectively creating high barriers to . . . trade. Thus, although there is a case to be made for temporary limited safeguard measures for developing countries with low import tariffs, in general, trade barriers on food make poor consumers less food secure, and even the temporary benefits to producers are debased in the longer run as the protectionism undermines more productive use of public and private investment resources and provokes reactive protection in other countries.

Apart from chronic food insecurity, there is a legitimate concern over temporary food supply disruptions caused by man-made or natural disasters, and this is sometimes used to justify protectionist measures to stimulate domestic food production. However, the impact of these disruptions could be mitigated through other measures, such as stockpiling of moderate reserves in cash or in kind, improving distribution channels, and reforming food aid, which would be more effective and less costly than efforts to stimulate food production. To the extent that disruptions stem from exporting countries restraining exports in times of high world prices, developing countries should act through the WTO to seek to constrain such behavior in the Doha agreement.

Real Solutions Will Raise Incomes

Because chronic food insecurity comes mainly from insufficient purchasing power of the poor, the real question is how the poor can be provided with opportunities to earn sufficient income so they can meet their consumption needs, regardless of whether they do so through food produced at home or abroad. Here, trade liberalization can have a major impact, as it would open markets for producers in developing countries not only to sell their products at higher prices, but also to buy better production technology, which in turn would help boost their productivity and raise their incomes. But this requires strong commitment from developing and industrialized countries to sweeping liberalization in the Doha trade negotiations. A successful Doha Round could produce huge benefits for the developing world and lift millions out of poverty. However, in the Doha talks, discussions of food security continue to center on domestic production, which is reflected in negotiating positions calling for more flexibility for developing countries—or some subset such as net food importing countries—to be exempted from the general obligations, so they can maintain high import barriers to food products under the rubric of "special products" or as a component of the "development box."

Rich countries' dumping of surplus production, billed as food aid, . . . undermines local food production and marketing channels.

The focus on domestic production may be a holdover from the past, when the global food distribution system was less developed, food imports were primarily the responsibility of often inefficient state enterprises, and poor macroeconomic policies created the specter of foreign exchange shortages at times when food imports were most needed. But under current conditions, the strategy should aim at reducing poverty, not increasing domestic food production. While a comprehensive strategy to fight hunger needs to have many components, including nutritional education, health infrastructure, safety nets, and more, the main determinant of undernutrition is income. Whereas it is difficult to find an example of a country where large numbers of people were lifted out of poverty but are still going hungry because of a lack of locally produced food, there are prominent cases of countries that are food self-sufficient at a national level—even holding large surplus stocks—but where large numbers of poor people continue to go hungry.

How Trade Liberalization Can Help

Clearly, when considering food security, the Doha trade liberalization talks need to shift the focus from how the trading system can be used to increase the degree of self-sufficiency to how it can help raise the incomes of the poor. In addition, to take advantage of the historic opportunity presented by the Round, the level of ambition in the negotiations needs to be ratcheted up. Developing countries can also take some unilateral steps that do not depend on the Round. The agenda should focus on these components, in rough order of priority:

- In a Doha Round agreement, all countries—rich and developing—should commit to lowering bound (ceiling) rates on food and other agricultural products to significantly reduce applied tariffs. This should be combined with a special safeguard or contingent protection mechanism for developing countries, which they can invoke in periods of exceptionally low world prices or import surges.

- Individual developing countries should enhance household food security by lowering applied tariffs on food product imports. To mitigate adverse effects on small producers who have limited resources to adjust, safety nets or transitional assistance schemes may be needed. While in principle such reforms are desirable even in the absence of multilateral negotiations, in practice they will be politically much easier if a successful agreement exists that calls for industrialized countries to reduce their own subsidies and border protection.

- Rural development strategies should focus policy, as well as productivity-enhancing investments and support services, on raising rural incomes and improving the environment for agricultural production in general (including exports), not on increasing food production. In many developing countries, agricultural investment needs to be increased, but in a way that creates a level playing field in which farmers can make unbiased production decisions.

- The practice of export taxation or controls by food-exporting countries in periods of high world prices should be restricted under the Doha Round agreement.

- Rich countries' dumping of surplus production, billed as food aid, in developing countries in periods of global gluts should also be disciplined in the agreement, as it undermines local food production and marketing channels.

- Developing countries should unilaterally lower regulatory and border barriers to trade in agricultural inputs such as seeds, fertilizers, chemicals, and equipment.

- Independently of the Doha Round, developing countries should lower barriers to cross-border regional trade in food products and invest in reducing the costs of this trade. Since shocks to the food supply are not perfectly correlated across neighboring countries, regional trade flows can help stabilize supplies and prices.

- Sweeping global trade liberalization could lead to a structural increase in global food prices, which could negatively impact poor consumers. However, there should be ample time for adjustment, as structural effects will appear gradually as agreements are implemented. In countries that currently impose tariffs on food imports, the domestic effect of higher world market prices can be offset by lowering tariffs. In other countries, safety nets may be needed to protect the most vulnerable. In addition, world prices will become less volatile, helping producers and consumers manage risks better. Nevertheless, a WTO panel is currently exploring ways to help poor consumers deal with potentially higher prices.

- The international trading system can clearly play a role in alleviating hunger, but governments and negotiators need to look beyond the short-term effects of protectionist barriers and work toward an open system that allows all people physical and economic access to sufficient, safe, and nutritious food.

Protecting Producers

Although part of the solution to food security is to eradicate import barriers, in periods of exceptionally low world prices, developing countries that agree to significantly lower WTO-bound tariffs should be allowed to invoke special temporary measures to protect production. While rich countries protect their producers from the high volatility in agricultural markets through safety nets of various kinds, the poorer countries cannot afford to do so. Thus, developing countries will be looking for other ways to protect producers of import-substitute crops.

Ideally, this should be done by direct payments not linked to how much input is used or how much output is produced, rather than an increase in import tariffs. But taking into consideration fiscal realities, it is likely that protection would have to come from tariffs. However, any tariff increases under this special mechanism should be time-bound, moderate in magnitude, and invoked only on rare occasions. Such constraints will at least minimize the inherent bias against exports that is created by protection. And this relatively neutral trade policy with no or modest protection for import substitutes would not hurt food production. In many countries, farmers traditionally follow a mixed-crop strategy, and the production of cash crops improves their ability to buy modern components for their food production. Hence, a positive empirical correlation exists between cash crop income and food production. This relationship is stronger in poorer countries, where non-farm income is more limited.

4

Free Trade Has Failed to Reduce World Hunger

Peter O'Driscoll

Peter O'Driscoll directs the Corporate Accountability Project and the Agribusiness Accountability Initiative at the Center of Concern, a Washington, D.C.–based Roman Catholic organization working for global peace and justice.

Since 1995 trade liberalization policies adopted by the World Trade Organization have increased global food trade to over 800 million tons annually. Yet the United Nations Food and Agriculture Organization reports that the number of hungry people in the world is up by 18 million over the same period of time. Although proponents of free trade argue that it will make food more affordable for everyone, in reality the policies benefit transnational agribusiness companies. They also increase rural poverty by depressing the prices that rural farmers, both in the United States and overseas, are able to receive for the crops they produce.

A huge proportion of the world's population still depends on subsistence farming or agricultural labor for its livelihood. Volatile climate conditions, long growing cycles and "information asymmetries" make it hard for farmers with limited resources to adapt quickly to market signals. Not surprisingly, poverty and malnutrition are most persistent in rural areas. Such factors lead many development experts to conclude that a judicious mix of government and market-based approaches

Peter O'Driscoll, "Part of the Problem: Trade, Transnational Corporations, and Hunger," *Center Focus*, no. 166, March 2005. Reproduced by permission.

must be applied to optimize food production and distribution and thereby reduce hunger.

But advocates of "free trade" have long resisted the argument that agriculture should be treated differently from other sectors of the economy, encouraging poor farmers instead to view tariff reduction and other liberalization measures as the best means to improve their prospects. Their views have definitely held sway in recent years. In 1995, the World Trade Organization [WTO] adopted an Agreement on Agriculture designed to accelerate global food trade. And when leaders gathered in Rome for the 1996 World Food Summit and pledged to halve the number of hungry people in the world by 2015, their final declaration included a commitment to "strive to ensure that food, agricultural trade and overall trade policies are conducive to fostering food security for all through a fair and market-oriented world trade system."

The Number of Hungry People Is Increasing

During the liberalization era, the volume of international agricultural trade has increased dramatically, growing four-fold over the past four decades to over 800 million tons per year. But who has benefited from this trend? Evidence suggests that agricultural trade liberalization has proven disastrous for developing countries, dislocating farmers and accelerating the concentration of land ownership. Moreover, the December 2004 report of the United Nations Food and Agriculture Organization on *The State of Food Insecurity* shows "the number of hungry people in the world rising to 852 million in 2000–2002, up by 18 million from the mid-1990s." The report's bottom line is sobering: a decade after the Agreement on Agriculture, and just a decade before the Food Summit's self-imposed 2015 deadline, the number of hungry people in the world is growing.

Agricultural trade liberalization's failure to deliver on the goal of reducing hunger is only one of several reasons why it has become a major stumbling block as the WTO attempts to push forward its "Doha Development Round." Countries of the global south oppose the hypocrisy that forces them to open their markets to U.S. and European agri-food companies without reciprocal access for their own exports. They note that food production in the developed world still receives government subsidies that poor countries are not allowed to offer their farmers, even if they could afford them.

Trade liberalization and monopoly power allow global processing companies . . . to force down the price of basic grains . . . worldwide.

Those subsidies will also be a major topic for domestic debate over the two years leading up to the 2007 Farm Bill. Forced by exploding budget deficits to seek cost savings wherever he can, President [George W.] Bush is proposing payment limitations on commodity subsidies to U.S. farmers. Some family farm groups here are ready to discuss subsidy reform in the context of broader efforts to combat the collapse of commodity prices. In solidarity with their colleagues in developing countries, they call for multilateral measures to guarantee fair prices to farmers everywhere, through supply management and the creation of strategic commodity reserves. But the prospects for implementing such reforms are limited by stiff opposition from the agribusiness lobby.

Agribusiness and the Price of Food

Raising the prices that farmers receive from their production would certainly address rural poverty and hunger. But it need not lead to higher food prices for consumers. Even as farm income has progressively declined, especially under "free trade" agreements, retail food prices have risen. In 1970, American farmers received 37 cents of every dollar spent on a market basket of food products, but by 2000 their share had fallen to 20 cents. The growing spread between farm revenue and consumer food prices has been driven by the market power of large agri-food companies. As explained by Dwayne Andreas, former chairman of Archer Daniels Midland Co. (ADM), "the food business is far and away the most important business in the world. Everything else is luxury." Because business is about making profit, food companies choose not to pass their cost savings from low-farm prices on to consumers.

Trade liberalization and monopoly power allow global processing companies like ADM and Cargill to force down the price of basic grains such as corn, wheat, rice and soy worldwide. Even as prices fall below the cost of production, farmers face a perverse incentive to increase their output to generate as much income as possible from a collapsing market, until they go out of business. In a vicious downward spiral of supply and demand, increased global production then drives farm prices even lower. Subsidies are lifelines that keep enough U.S. farmers on this production treadmill to guarantee continued low prices to the processing companies.

Subsidy payments ensure continued overproduction and low commodity prices because 60% of the U.S. subsidy budget goes to the largest 10% of farmers. Processing companies "dump" much of their subsidized cheap grain onto developing country markets, discouraging local production and gaining effective control of grain distribution. But even as American and European taxpayers subsidize farmers to maximize agribusiness profits in the name of "free trade," the companies themselves know better. ADM's Andreas acknowledged that "there isn't one grain of anything in the world that is sold in a free market. Not one! The only place you see a free market is in the speeches of politicians."

Corporate control of food policy and agricultural trade has been locked in by two factors: the industry's extraordinary access to policymakers (often through "revolving door" appointments of executives to key government posts), and the degree of market concentration in the food system. Big companies are not shy about their political influence. Cargill's Chief Executive Warren Staley acknowledged [in 2004] that "when we suggest to someone we have an issue and would like to meet them, the doors are almost always open because of the courteous manner in which we approach things, and our credibility." Such influence was exemplified by the April 2003 appointment of former Cargill Vice-President Dan Amstutz to lead agricultural reconstruction efforts in Iraq. It was Amstutz who had "drafted the original text of the current Uruguay Round Agreement on Agriculture within the World Trade Organization, considered by many developing countries and pro-development groups as innately unjust. The agreement allows rich countries to dump their subsidy-backed agricultural surpluses on world markets, depressing prices to levels at which producers in developing nations can no longer compete." Amstutz quickly used his authority to commit Iraq to controversial laws that forbid farmers to save seeds and thus produce a financial windfall for seed companies like Monsanto—an important business partner for Cargill.

Corporate Control of the Food System

As if the capacity to shape government policy were not enough, agri-food firms also use old-fashioned monopoly power to exert their control: in the absence of competition, they can fix prices both to farmers and consumers. A handful of companies now dominate every sector of the food system, from inputs like seeds, pesticides and fertilizers, through the processing and manufacturing of food products, all the way to retail and food service. Just two companies (Monsanto and DuPont) together dominate global seed markets for maize (65%) and soy (44%). Seventy-five per cent of all human food is grain-based, yet three companies (Cargill, Archer Daniels

Midland and Bunge) control about 90% of the global grain trade. Over the past 20 years, the proportion of U.S. production controlled by the four largest firms has risen from 60% to 82% in beef packing, from 30% to 57% for pork, and from 54% to 80% in soybean crushing, to name a few key agricultural markets. Meanwhile, more than 300,000 U.S. family farms were lost over that same period.

Important voices are becoming alarmed by this trend. The U.S. Catholic Bishops noted in November 2003 that as a result of "increasing concentration at every level of agriculture . . . fewer people are making important decisions that affect far more people than in the past. . . . These forces of increasing concentration and growing globalization are pushing . . . us toward a world where the powerful can take advantage of the weak, where large institutions and corporations can overwhelm smaller structures, and where the production and distribution of food and the protection of land lie in fewer hands."

Pointing out that the quest for monopoly profits can lead companies to constrain food access for poor people, United Nations Special Rapporteur Jean Ziegler affirmed in October 2003 that "despite the fact that Transnational Corporations increasingly control our food system, there are still relatively few mechanisms in place to ensure that they respect standards and do not violate human rights." Even the mainstream press has begun to focus on the problem. The editorial page of the *New York Times* declared [in] December [2004] that "it is essential to reverse the trend toward concentration in American farming."

Looking for Solutions

Key stakeholder groups are similarly concerned. Since 2002, in partnership with the National Catholic Rural Life Conference, the Center of Concern has been building the Agribusiness Accountability Initiative (AAI) into an international network of representatives from farm, labor, consumer, environment, church and development groups willing to work together to confront the political influence and market power of transnational agri-food companies. Hosting forum events in Chicago, Kansas City, London, Brussels and Sao Paulo, AAI has convened over 300 civil society leaders from more than 30 countries to share their analysis of food industry issues, to support each other's existing reform efforts, and to create new cross-constituency research and advocacy to promote a more socially, politically and environmentally sustainable food system.

AAI Forums have already achieved important results. The October 2003 Forum in Kansas City launched a cross-sectoral working group to expose industry influence on U.S. agri-food policy, leading to the July 2004 publication of *USDA Inc.— How Agribusiness has Hijacked Regulatory Policy at the U.S. Department of Agriculture*. AAI then reached out to groups exploring conflict of interest in other federal agencies, and has now formed a broad coalition to create ethics laws that prevent "revolving door" appointments.

The Kansas City forum also set up a committee of food industry researchers to create a web-accessible matrix, showing which companies control what percentage of key agri-food markets around the world. AAI convened 24 researchers from around the world in Paris in January [2005] to share data, launch the matrix, and propose a plan for ongoing research. Meanwhile, the AAI Forum in Brussels in January 2004 led to the formation of a continent-wide coalition of groups working to create European Union regulations to limit the monopoly power of supermarkets. . . .

While food may be a "business" to Dwayne Andreas, those who see it primarily as a basic human right, as it is designated in Catholic social teaching texts, must work together to guarantee that food is available to all who need it—not just to those who can afford to pay a corporate premium.

5

A History of U.S. Food Aid

Ryan Swanson

Ryan Swanson is with the Federal Research Division of the Library of Congress.

The United States has a long history, going back to World War I (1914–1918), of supplying humanitarian food assistance around the world. The Berlin Airlift of 1948, the Marshall Plan, Food for Peace, the Agricultural Trade Act of 1980, Food for Progress, and the McGovern-Dole International Food for Education and Child Nutrition Program are all examples of ways in which the United States has responded effectively to the problem of hunger worldwide.

The numbers are startling. More than 800 million people go to bed hungry each night, and nearly 50 million people currently face acute hunger as a result of war, civil strife or natural disaster. Additionally, the United Nations estimates that malnutrition is a significant factor in the deaths of 11,000 children each day.

Even in the 21st century, with its technological advances, the quest for food security remains a daunting challenge. There is some reason for optimism, however, as the United States and many other countries have put in place programs to fight hunger throughout the world and significant success has been achieved. But even with these victories, there is still much work yet to be done.

Ryan Swanson, "Fighting World Hunger: U.S. Food Aid Policy and the Food for Peace Movement," *AgExporter*, vol. 16, October 2004, p. 4. Copyright 2004 U.S. Department of Agriculture. Reproduced by permission.

Although fertile soil and proficient farmers have consistently provided for the United States' domestic food needs, U.S. leaders have long recognized that the problem of food scarcity knows no national borders. On one hand, basic humanitarianism demands that hunger elsewhere cannot be simply ignored. But also, and perhaps more practically speaking, today's international economy determines that problems rarely stay confined to one particular country or region. The reverberations of food scarcity in one country make their impact felt in food markets around the world. The U.S. government designates millions of dollars and tons of food each year for food aid.

A Long History of Providing Food Aid

The United States has a long history of providing assistance to needy countries around the world. Following World War I, the American Relief Administration, led by entrepreneur and soon-to-be president Herbert Hoover, distributed more than 4 million tons of food and supplies to starving people in Europe, especially the Soviet Union. The Berlin Airlift of 1948 came in response to [Soviet leader] Joseph Stalin's closure of all roads and railroads into Berlin in June 1948. For nearly one year, British and American forces responded by delivering by plane all food and other necessary materials to sustain the isolated city. The delivery of over 500,000 tons of food eventually broke Stalin's blockade.

Although food aid programs currently enjoy widespread political support, it took a war to open the eyes of many politicians regarding their importance. World War II pushed the United States to increase and formalize its food aid efforts. Throughout the years of fighting, Congress approved the donation of thousands of tons of food to European allies, especially the Soviet Union, to support both their armies and civilians. These food donations saved thousands of lives as famine spread throughout Europe. Following the war, U.S. involvement in food aid efforts continued to increase. The Marshall Plan, totaling nearly $13 billion, focused on feeding victims of the war and rebuilding the infrastructure and economy of Western Europe and Japan.

It was through this Plan, named for Secretary of State George C. Marshall, that U.S. government and military leaders first gained valuable experience in distributing food aid to destitute people. These leaders demonstrated to American politicians that a massive aid program could benefit both recipients and givers.

Chief among these rising leaders was a young army officer named Gwynn Garnett. Garnett served as the director of food and agriculture in the American zone of Germany and, on a daily basis, oversaw the procurement and distribution of extraordinary amounts of food to needy citizens. In this role, Garnett solidified an idea that changed U.S. food aid. Garnett proposed that the United States accept foreign currencies, many of which were virtually worthless outside their own borders after the war, in exchange for U.S. agricultural products. Although this approach seemed to suggest that the United States take a "loss" on its exports, Garnett focused on the larger ramifications.

The United States could use the local currency to rebuild the infrastructure and markets of war-ravaged areas that needed food. The United States could also fund the donation of food to the truly destitute. This investment would, in turn, facilitate the reopening of valuable markets for U.S. producers.

Leaders in both the [Dwight D.] Eisenhower Administration and Congress quickly embraced Garnett's plan when he presented it upon returning from Germany to serve as an American Farm Bureau official. The plan proved to be popular on two levels. It provided a structure by which the United States could meet the growing food needs of the world, and it helped put surplus U.S. agricultural production to good use.

The Foreign Agricultural Service and Food for Peace

The Agricultural Trade Development and Assistance Act of 1954 stamped Congress' approval on Garnett's plan. After the passage of P.L. (Public Law) 480 in July 1954, USDA [U.S. Department of Agriculture] received its marching orders. The law provided the means to offer needy countries low-interest, long-term credit to purchase U.S. agricultural goods. The President delegated the concessional credit authority under that Act to the Secretary of Agriculture, who re-delegated that authority to FAS [the Foreign Agricultural Service].

P.L. 480, which has six program titles, continues 50 years after its origin to be the backbone of the United States' diverse food aid effort. Administered by FAS, Title I makes available long-term, low interest credit to needy countries so that they may purchase U.S. agricultural commodities. Title I allows the long-term debt acquired under P.L. 480 to be repaid in the currency of the borrowing country; however, since the early 1970s, P.L. 480 debt has been repaid in U.S. dollars.

For countries where even the most generous credit terms are too heavy an economic burden, U.S. efforts take a different approach. Title II of P.L. 480, administered by USAID (the U.S. Agency for International Development), allows for the outright donation of U.S. agricultural commodities to meet humanitarian needs around the world. Donations can be distributed through government agencies, private charities or international organizations such as the WFP (World Food Program).

Commodities are currently obtained by purchase from private producers or from stocks held by USDA's CCC (Commodity Credit Corporation). In addition, the Title II program pays the transport, storage and distribution costs associated with the donations. Title III of P.L. 480, the Food for Development program, is currently inactive. Also administered by USAID, it provides government-to-government assistance grants to least-developed countries to support development.

Drawing on a Heritage of Aiding the Needy

P.L. 480 built upon the Agricultural Act of 1949, which allowed excess commodities held by the CCC to be distributed outside the United States when the need arose. In 1951 alone, Congress acted to help Yugoslavia and India through times of famine. The Yugoslav Emergency Relief Assistance Act in 1951 had particular significance because it sent an important message of support to Yugoslavia as it broke ties with the Soviet Union.

As is the case with most legislation, the true impact of P.L. 480 became evident as details became codified and action commenced. Initially, politicians argued over how exactly the program would function. Senator Hubert Humphrey, in particular, championed the idea that P.L. 480 must emphasize the donation of food to needy countries, and that such efforts must not exist only as a side-note to surplus commodity disposal. In his 1958 Congressional report entitled "'Food and Fiber as a Force for Freedom," Humphrey took issue with farmers whom he felt were interested only in surplus reallocation for the benefit of American agriculturalists.

> *Food aid policy must . . . preserve the normal flow of trade and . . . limit any price impact on agricultural commodities.*

Eventually, President Dwight D. Eisenhower pursued a middle road that took into consideration both the plight of American farmers and the vast potential of food diplomacy. The President supported Humphrey's call for P.L. 480 to be known as the "Food for Peace program," and in 1960 established both the position of Food for Peace Coordinator and the Office of Food for Peace.

U.S. food aid policy evolved continuously as new needs arose, new challenges cropped up, and different presidential administrations placed their stamp on aid efforts. In 1961, President John F. Kennedy established USAID. The new Agency partnered with FAS in the disbursal of food aid throughout the world, and it continues to administer Title II distributions. In 1962, in response to appeals that had been made by both Eisenhower and Kennedy, the United Nations established its WFP. At the suggestion of Senator George McGovern, who was then the White House Director of the U.S. Food for Peace program, the WFP began initially on a three-year trial basis before rapidly assuming a permanent, leading role in the fight to reduce hunger.

The Food Aid Convention of 1967 brought the question of how to confront world hunger to the forefront of international relations. For the first time, the United States and 11 other developed countries gathered to discuss their mutual commitments to food aid. The participating government leaders reached a formal agreement that set minimum levels of food support for needy countries each year, regardless of surpluses or commodity prices that might be in effect. The United States assumed by far the largest responsibility, originally providing over 75 percent of the commodities donated, but a precedent of international cooperation was established.

Ever-Increasing Challenges

As support for food aid policies has expanded, logistical challenges have increased as well. Early FAS and USAID administrators faced the challenge of deciding which countries should be served; how excess commodities should be obtained; and which commodities were most suitable nutritionally. Other questions, such as how the cost of transport should be met and how aid should be distributed without altering the world trade balance, also presented significant challenges.

Food aid policy must be carefully constructed in order to preserve the normal flow of trade and to limit any price impact on agricultural commodities. FAS officials closely observe usual marketing requirements, mandating that countries receiving aid continue to trade even as they receive outside assistance. FAS prohibits the resale of P.L. 480 Title I commodities to third countries. P.L. 480 Title I requires that all purchases go through a rigorous bidding system. The recipient governments make the purchases. FSA (the Farm Service Agency) of USDA purchases commodities for Title II using an open competitive process. Additionally, P.L. 480 protects the ability of small businesses to participate by disallowing minimum order levels under Title II. These rules exist to create competition and integrity on the supply side in order that food aid needs can be met as efficiently and prudently as possible.

New challenges arise each year. Recently, U.S. efforts to assist countries in need of food have been plagued by controversy over the use of biotechnology. FAS and USAID officials have taken on the role of educator as they explain why and how this technology is used. Adding to the changes, the scope of food aid has continued to evolve. The new goal of food security encompasses more than just donations in times of crisis. Rather, "food security" focuses on the access by all people at all times to sufficient food for active, healthy lives.

Adaptation and Flexibility Are Key to Success

Because of the constantly changing landscape of food needs around the world, U.S. food aid policy has come to be characterized by continual evolution of many different programs. While P.L. 480 still functions quite effectively, the U.S. government has added new programs to address previously unforeseen situations. In the 1980s, food aid officials recognized that in order for the United States to have the freedom to address pressing international needs as they arise, an adequate reserve was needed. A commodity reserve, originally authorized by the Agricultural Trade Act of 1980 and now known as the Bill Emerson Humanitarian Trust, serves that purpose by allowing the United States to store up to 4 million metric tons of wheat, corn, sorghum and rice, to be used in case of a food emergency or to otherwise meet P.L. 480 program needs in a tight supply situation. The Secretary of Agriculture has authority to release up to 500,000 tons of grain each year for emergency assistance.

Numerous times throughout the 1980s and 1990s, presidents have released grain from the Trust in response to difficult circumstances. In 1984, President Ronald Reagan authorized the release of 300,000 tons of grain to help fight widespread famine in Africa. Presidents George H.W. Bush and Bill Clinton designated the release of grain to aid the Middle East and the Caucasus regions. In 2002, officials released 275,000 tons of grain to again aid starving people in Southern Africa. The drought in that region created a situation of unexpected severity, the type of unpredictable calamity that the Emerson Trust was intended to hedge against. The fund currently has a balance of over 2 million tons.

Food for Progress

In the 1980s, another significant new food aid program emerged, this one with a more concerted diplomatic focus. The Food for Progress initiative, first authorized in 1985, made very explicit the connection between the donation of food and the recipient country's philosophy of government. Commodities came from CCC stocks or purchases from the market and may be furnished in the form of either financing or donations.

But most significantly, Food for Progress did just what its title suggested—it linked food and progress. Only countries that were emerging democracies or that made a significant commitment to free enterprise in their agricultural economies could receive aid under this provision.

Food for Progress donations have been made to countries all over the world. In 1999, for example, after Hurricane Mitch nearly crippled Honduras and Nicaragua, FAS, through the Food for Progress program, made direct food donations valued in excess of $13.5 million. The donations eased the hunger caused by the hurricane and helped with the rebuilding of the agricultural infrastructure in those countries.

The legacy of U.S. efforts ... will provide a strong foundation to continue to work toward food security.

Like the Food for Progress initiative, the most recent addition to the United States' array of food aid programs seeks to improve the societal conditions of the receiving country. In July 2000, President Bill Clinton committed the United States to providing resources worth $300 million to help establish school nutrition programs in needy countries. Strongly backing this move were two long-time proponents of food aid and increased school nutrition programs, Senators George McGovern and Robert Dole. In 2001, the pilot Global Food for Education Initiative began distributing commodities via the WFP as well as through many private voluntary organizations.

In the course of a two-year trial, the program provided nutritional meals for nearly 7 million children in 38 countries. The goal was not only to abate hunger, but also to increase the number of children who attend school; it is estimated that 12.1 million school-age children currently do not attend school because of lack of food and proper nutrition. Many are forced to work in the fields to maintain even a subsistence lifestyle.

This new initiative gained permanent status under the 2002 Farm Security and Rural Investment Act. As a result of the legislation, the McGovern-Dole International Food for Education and Child Nutrition Program was launched in 2003 to provide school meals, teacher training and technological support to foreign countries. The program will take different forms in different countries. In Eritrea, for example, plans call for a joint program to be conducted through Africare and Mercy Corps International to provide 65,000 students with high-protein biscuits and milk throughout the school year. In Guatemala, Catholic Relief Services and World Share will take profits made from selling U.S. goods and use them to purchase locally grown food in order to supplement students' diets. In addition to the program flexibility that allows different organizations to distribute aid, the McGovern-Dole program also pays transport and shipping costs.

Undoubtedly, new challenges will arise in the coming years. Changes in technology, the environment and the economy will cause food aid policymakers to seek new ways to help feed the hungry around the world. But the legacy of U.S. efforts such as Food for Peace and Food for Progress will provide a strong foundation to continue to work toward food security for the world's most vulnerable citizens.

6

Food Aid Is Failing to Address the Problem of World Hunger

Shahla Shapouri and Stacey Rosen

Shahla Shapouri and Stacey Rosen are staff members of the U.S. Department of Agriculture's Economic Research Service.

In recent years, the international community has failed to meet its goals for reducing food insecurity. Among the reasons for unmet goals are increased demand due to population growth, slow growth in food production, lack of purchasing power, and natural and human-made disasters in the world's neediest countries. Also, donor nations have reduced market supports for agriculture in recent years, resulting in decreases in the agricultural surpluses that have historically made food aid possible. Even in situations where available food quantities are adequate to meet needs, poor distribution systems can render food aid ineffective in addressing actual needs. The result is that food aid programs are increasingly failing to meet existing needs.

In 1996, the World Food Summit set its sights on reducing by half the number of hungry people in the world by 2015. But 8 years after the signing of this declaration, the international community is coming to grips with the fact that it will fall far short of its goal. All indicators developed by ERS [Economic Research Service] lead to the inescapable conclusion that the aggregate food security situation—measured by food

Shahla Shapouri and Stacey Rosen, "Fifty Years of U.S. Food Aid and Its Role in Reducing World Hunger," *Amber Waves*, September 2004. Reproduced by permission.

availability of many low-income countries—has hardly improved at all [since the 1990s]. Reports from the Food and Agriculture Organization (FAO) of the United Nations tell the same story.

Among the reasons for chronic undernutrition in the poorest countries are slow growth in domestic food production, high population growth, inadequate purchasing power, and frequent setbacks associated with natural and manmade shocks, such as drought, hurricanes, and civil strife. To counter the trend, the ultimate goal is to reduce the impacts of shocks, which reduce food production and consume too many resources in countries with too few to spare. Until that long-term goal can be met, it is critical to strengthen the food safety net in the most vulnerable countries. Because most poor countries do not have national food safety net programs, they depend on international food aid. But food aid increasingly falls short of needs: quantities change annually, and overall levels have grown only minimally during the life of the programs. The uncertain availability of food aid, though worrisome, is just one reason why food aid has not played a larger role in reducing world hunger. Differing objectives in food aid programs, lack of consistency among donors' approaches to food aid, and types of food donated are just a few factors that limit the effectiveness (the degree to which it reduces a country's food gaps) of food aid.

The Future of Food Aid Programs Is Uncertain

The global quantity of food aid has fluctuated during the last two decades, and its share has declined relative to both total agricultural exports from food aid suppliers and total food imports of low-income countries. The virtual stagnation in the level of food aid over time is not likely to change, and it may even decline if budgets remain tight. As major donor nations reduce market support to agriculture due to budget constraints as well as to comply with their commitments to the World Trade Organization, decreases in surplus food production will likely follow. The costs of food aid may increase as a result.

As the trend in supplies of food aid has remained relatively flat, the gap between food production and food consumption in low-income countries, and thus the demand for food aid, has widened. According to ERS, the gap between recommended nutritional requirements and purchasing power of the populations in the world's poorest countries was more than 32 million tons in 2003, about four times larger than the supply of food aid in 2002. While this gap is projected to narrow to less than 28 million tons during the next decade, it will likely remain far above the level of available food aid, which may decline.

According to the World Bank, about 1 billion people in developing countries live in poverty with annual per capita incomes of less than $370. In some regions, particularly Sub-Saharan Africa, per capita food consumption has declined in the last two decades, but food aid supplies have not changed since the late 1980s. For these countries, further declines in food consumption from already low levels can lead to severe food shortages, malnutrition, and political instability.

Ideally, the volume of food aid would have matched the consumption shortfalls. In practice, however, food aid followed a declining trend.

These estimates, however, do not necessarily mean that significant increases in food aid would be able to close these gaps. Given the poor distribution systems in these countries, absorption of large quantities of food imports would be difficult, if not impossible. Nevertheless, targeting efforts in the distribution of food aid need to be improved in order to increase its effectiveness and reduce hunger. There are growing and unresolved questions related to the impacts and the role of food aid. Despite 50 years of food donations, food aid's role in reducing world hunger remains unclear.

How Effective Is Food Aid?

There are three types of food aid, each with a differing objective. *Program food aid* is a government-to-government donation that aims to reduce food import costs for the recipient country. *Project food aid* is used by a government or nongovernment organization to provide support for development projects. *Emergency food aid* is used to augment food supplies or assist in rebuilding productive assets for countries affected by political or natural disasters.

The different uses of food aid have generated debates on the positive (additional food supplies) and negative (production disincentive due to the decline in local prices) effects of the programs. Still, food aid is regarded as a valuable resource for increasing food consumption by providing temporary relief from food shortages. But has food aid reduced consumption instability over time? Since the quantities of food aid fall short of the aggregate needs of the study countries, the next question is whether food aid is provided to those who need it the most.

What does food aid contribute to consumption? The overall contribution of food aid to total food consumption in the 70 countries included in ERS's annual Food Security Assessment is small, but the importance of food aid is more pronounced when it is measured at the country level at particular points in time. The 70 countries covered in this exercise include 4 in North Africa, 37 in Sub-Saharan Africa, 10 in Asia, 11 in Latin America and the Caribbean, and 8 in the Commonwealth of Independent States (CIS). Food aid, on average, provided less than 4 percent of food consumption (grain equivalent) for the

70 countries in the last decade, but the share varied greatly by country and tended to be more significant during emergencies.

- During Somalia's 1992–93 civil war, food aid contributed to about 70 percent of its consumption.

- When Mozambique was faced with prolonged economic and political difficulties (early 1980s through early 1990s), it often relied on food aid to supplement more than a third of its food consumption.

- In Rwanda during 1997–99, food aid contributed to more than a third of food consumption.

- Since 2000, Eritrea has relied on food aid for about half of its consumption.

- During 2000–02, the largest recipients of food aid were North Korea (4.2 million tons total for the 3 years), Ethiopia (4.0 million tons), Bangladesh (1.4 million tons), and Afghanistan (1.1 million tons). In North Korea, food aid contributed to about 20 percent of food consumption. In Ethiopia and Bangladesh, food aid's contribution to consumption was less than 10 percent.

Has food aid stabilized consumption? Food aid clearly had a significant role in reducing the loss of life during food emergencies in such countries as Ethiopia, Sudan, Somalia, Afghanistan, Rwanda, and Haiti. However, over time and at the aggregate level, the impact was less apparent. Based on food consumption data (grain only) in 62 low-income countries, the annual consumption shortfalls from trends in each country (excluding food aid) during 1981–99 exceeded the cumulative quantity of food aid received over the same period by 8 percent. Ideally, the volume of food aid would have matched the consumption shortfalls. In practice, however, food aid followed a declining trend while consumption shortfalls varied annually: in 5 of the 19 years, aggregate food aid exceeded the consumption shortfalls; in 12 of the years, it was less than the shortfalls; and in only 2 years (1986 and 1992) did the quantities match. The comparisons are much more uneven at the country level.

Does food aid respond to needs? The effectiveness of food aid depends on whether it is provided to those who need it most. *Distribution food gaps*, as estimated by ERS, reflect the amount of food needed to raise consumption of all income groups within a country to the nutritional requirement. This measure captures the differences in purchasing power within a country. *Food aid effectiveness* is measured on a scale of 0 to 100 percent, with 0 percent reflecting food aid given to a country with no needs and 100 percent reflecting food aid that reduces a country's food gap by its full amount. This method measures actual consumption as related to purchasing power within the countries at the national level and may not capture micro-level specific programs, such as food for work, which could be location specific.

During 1991–2000, the average effectiveness of food aid was 66 percent, meaning two-thirds of food aid went toward reducing and/or eliminating the recipient countries' food gaps. The remaining 34 percent went to countries that either did not have food needs or that had needs less than the amount of food actually received. Regionally, food aid deliveries in Sub-Saharan Africa and Latin America were highly effective in reducing food gaps, averaging about 80 percent, compared with 40–46 percent in Asia and the CIS.

The effectiveness of food aid in meeting nutritional needs depends highly on how food aid is allocated and what criteria are used to make allocation decisions. The largest nutritional gain is realized when food aid is targeted to the lowest income group—thus indirectly increasing this group's purchasing power—either in emergency situations or in support of supplementary feeding programs, such as food stamps. In these cases, food aid changes a country's income distribution indirectly because it allows the lower income group to consume more than expected given its income level. In 2000, about half of food aid was used for emergencies, which can be categorized as targeted. It is not clear how much of the other half was targeted—the effectiveness of other uses of food aid in reducing hunger is difficult to estimate. All food aid reduces food costs in the market, making food more affordable; but without targeting to the most vulnerable group, the benefits of food aid tend to be distributed across the entire population of a country.

Many Reasons for Failure

There are many unresolved issues relating to food aid. After 50 years, there are neither uniform approaches nor transparent criteria among donors regarding decisions to allocate food aid. Program eligibility criteria are loosely defined, and it is not always clear when an activity stops, and why. Many countries receive food aid for reasons that are not clear. For example, China received wheat in 2000–02 as food aid to finance development projects, but, in turn, donated food (wheat, rice, corn, oils) to North Korea and several African countries during the same period. In addition, it is not clear what governs donor decisions to shift from the use of food aid for development purposes to emergency relief (or vice versa) both within a country and across countries. Such changes have implications (positive or negative) on the coordination and management of food aid between donors and recipients. In each case, it is difficult to measure which potential goals are met (cost effectiveness, meeting recipient needs) and to what extent. Compounding the problem are the changes in annual availability of food aid stemming from donors' political and budgetary considerations. It is an open question whether a program with this type of characteristic can provide a reliable food safety net, let alone a reliable source of development.

Another issue of concern is the producer disincentive impact of food aid when it is sold for development activities. In such cases, food aid results in lower producer prices, which reduces incentives to produce, thereby creating a growing dependency on food aid. The selection of commodities used for food aid is also raising questions. The growing share of noncereal food aid products, such as vegetable oil, pasta, dried potatoes, dried fish, pulses [legumes], sugar, and fresh vegetables, is potentially worrisome. As recently as the early 1990s, these products accounted for only 9 percent of total food aid donations; 10 years later, the share had jumped to more than 14 percent. This is problematic because these commodities are higher priced than cereals and, therefore, are not likely to reach the poorest segment of the population. In some cases, these commodities now account for a larger share of the food aid package than cereals. For example, in 2000, noncereals accounted for two-thirds of Georgia's food aid receipts (67,739 tons in grain equivalent).

Improving the Effectiveness of Food Aid

The goal of the World Food Summit was to halve global hunger in a little over a decade. Each and every signatory country bears the responsibility of meeting this goal, but short-term economic and political shocks around the world remain serious obstacles. The United States plays a pivotal role within the international food aid system, and its actions have a profound effect on the actions of other donors and the system as a whole. The 50th anniversary of the U.S. food aid program in 2004 [was] a timely point to appraise the program and reexamine plans for the future. The U.S. *Action Plan on Food Security*, released in March 1999, outlines policies and actions aimed at alleviating hunger at home and abroad. To improve the effectiveness of the international food assistance program, the action plan made aid to the most food-insecure countries a priority. It is too early to evaluate the impacts of this policy change, but steps are being taken by the U.S. Government to develop transparent methods to monitor the effectiveness of food aid in reducing hunger in recipient countries.

The impact of food aid in reducing hunger has fallen short of its potential and, in some cases, has negatively affected the economies of the recipient countries.

Lessons from the past could be useful toward improving the effectiveness of food aid. For example, emergency food aid has saved lives (response to drought in Ethiopia, 1984–85, 1991, 1999–2000, and Zambia, 1992; response to civil strife in Somalia, 1991–92, and Rwanda, mid-late 1990s; response to Hurricane Mitch in Honduras in 1998–99; response to financial crisis in Indonesia in 1998). Food aid has also proved effective in post-emergency situations.

Other uses of food aid, however, have had mixed results, particularly program food aid, that is, government-to-government donations that are commonly sold in recipient country markets. Program food aid is a resource transfer and is often used to reduce financial constraints of recipient countries. Therefore, it is not targeted to any specific nutritional or development objectives. Another drawback of program food aid is the potential for interfering with market functions. The most prevalent food aid commodities are cereals and vegetable oils, commodities most often imported commercially by the recipient. The injection of food aid in this circumstance can disrupt markets and depress producer prices.

There is also evidence that program food aid, in some instances, has created structural import dependency. For example, program food aid has encouraged the development of industries, such as poultry farming or wheat milling, that require imports to continue operations even after the termination of the food aid program.

Overall, the impact of food aid in reducing hunger has fallen short of its potential and, in some cases, has negatively affected the economies of the recipient countries. A more important problem lies in the fact that there is no coordination among donors to establish guidelines for distribution and need-based targeting of food aid. It is an annual budgetary program, which hinders its flexibility to expand or contract in response to the needs of recipients. However, steps toward transparent goals and criteria for food aid eligibility, length of the program, and type of program could enhance its effectiveness and pave the road to improved coordination among donors.

7

Genetic Engineering Can Help Solve the Problem of World Hunger

Jorge E. Mayer, Peter Beyer, and Ingo Potrykus

Jorge E. Mayer, Peter Beyer, and Ingo Potrykus are the developers of a genetically engineered cereal grain called Golden Rice. Mayer and Beyer are faculty members at the University of Freiburg in Germany. Potrykus is professor emeritus at the Federal Institute of Technology (ETH Institute) for Plant Science in Zurich, Switzerland.

Millions of children die every year as a result of malnutrition. One way to decrease the number of deaths is through biofortification—the use of gene technology to enrich the nutritional value of traditional staple crops. One example of biofortification is Golden Rice, which has been genetically improved to contain beta-carotene, an essential nutrient necessary for the synthesis of vitamin A. Biofortification is the easiest and most cost-effective way to reduce micronutrient malnutrition among the world's poorest people.

In the year 2000, more than 792 million people in 98 developing countries did not get enough food to lead a normal, healthy and active life, as estimated by FAO [United Nations Food and Agriculture Organization]. Nine million children die of malnutrition every year; a vast majority of these deaths is linked to micronutrient deficiencies. The deficiencies with the highest impact on morbidity and mortality are in iron, zinc, iodine and vitamin A.

At its inception, the Golden Rice Project set out to alleviate the vitamin A deficiency (VAD) problem, because of its relevance and potential impact. Yearly, half a million people—mainly children—become blind as a consequence of VAD, 50 percent of which die within a year of becoming blind. VAD severely affects the immune system; hence it is also involved in many of these children's deaths in the guise of various infectious diseases. Recently, malaria deaths in children under five years of age have been linked to deficiencies in intake of protein, vitamin A and zinc. Various public and international programmes working on supplementation, fortification and diet diversification have achieved substantial improvements but have difficulty in attaining full coverage of the affected population and above all, sustainability. Biofortification—the fortification of crop tissues by means of their own biosynthetic capacity—involves conventional breeding of genetically improved staple crops, and offers an opportunity to obtain a more inclusive coverage, especially of the poorest sectors of society. Genetic improvement can be achieved in various ways, including conventional selection, introgression of traits from wild relatives, mutagenesis and genetic engineering.

Rice Eaters Become Vitamin A Deficient

VAD is prevalent among the poor who depend mainly on rice for their daily energy intake, because the rice endosperm—the starchy, edible part of the rice grains—does not contain any beta-carotene (provitamin A), which our body could then convert into vitamin A. Dependence on rice as the predominant food source, therefore, necessarily leads to VAD, most severely affecting children and pregnant women. For the 400 million rice-consuming poor, the medical consequences are severe: impaired vision, in extreme cases irreversible blindness, impaired epithelial integrity, exposing the affected individuals to infections, reduced immune response, impaired hematopoiesis [ability to make red blood cells] and skeletal growth, among other debilitating afflictions. Rice containing beta-carotene could substantially reduce the problem. This can only be achieved using genetic engineering because there is no provitamin A in the endosperm, even though it is produced in the leaves of rice plants. No variability for this trait, suitable for breeding purposes, has been detected in the world's most important rice germplasm collections.

Biofortification . . . is presumably the most sustainable and cost-effective approach to reduce micronutrient malnutrition.

Golden Rice has been engineered to contain the genes necessary to make up the biochemical pathway for beta-carotene production in the grain. This breakthrough achievement was the result of many years of work by Ingo Potrykus and Peter Beyer, in Switzerland and Germany, respectively. The only thing required to turn on the pathway, which is silent in the grain, is to add two genes. These two genes were borrowed originally from daffodils and from *Erwinia uredovora*, a soil bacterium. Since the breakthrough in the year 1999, the gene construct was further refined to be expressed exclusively in the rice endosperm. In 2005, [biotech firm] Syngenta scientists were capable of increasing the beta-carotene level obtained in the first-generation Golden Rice 23-fold, by replacing the daffodil with a homologous gene from maize. This level of beta-carotene should be enough to cover the recommended daily requirements of children and adults in rice-based societies.

Reaching Out

Golden Rice will be made available to developing countries within the framework of a humanitarian project. This was, from the onset, a public research project designed to reduce malnutrition in developing countries. Thanks to strong support from the private sector and free licences for humanitarian use, the hurdle of extensive intellectual property rights attached to the technologies used in the production of Golden Rice could be overcome early during the process. The arrangement opened the way to collaborations with public rice research institutions in developing countries, providing freedom to operate to develop locally adapted Golden Rice varieties.

Once locally developed rice varieties containing the Golden trait have gone through regulatory approval—including all required biosafety testing—at the national level, seed will be made available to subsistence farmers, free of charge. The seed will become their property and they will also be able to use part of their harvest for the next sowing, without restrictions. Golden Rice is compatible with the use of traditional farming systems, not requiring additional agronomic inputs. Therefore, no new dependencies will be created. Moreover, as concluded by many experts, the Golden trait does not pose any conceivable risk to the environment which would justify delaying its widespread use.

The progress achieved since the initial breakthrough would not have been possible without an innovative type of public-private partnership. Thanks to an agreement with Syngenta and other agbiotech industries, Golden Rice is royalty-free for humanitarian use, which, for the purpose of this project, is defined as 'an annual farm income in the range of US$10,000 per farmer, while a higher income would require a commercial licence from Syngenta.' Royalty-free humanitarian sublicences are granted by the Golden Rice Humanitarian Board to public rice research institutions. These sublicence agreements ensure that the material is handled according to established biosafety guidelines and regulations, and that the target population—subsistence farmers and the urban poor—receives the biofortified rice with no surcharge for the Golden trait.

Tailored for Local Consumption

Development of locally adapted Golden Rice varieties and applications to national authorities for field testing and for regulatory approval is in the hands of national and international public rice research institutions. To date, the Golden Rice Network includes eighteen national, developing-country institutions in Bangladesh, China, India, Indonesia, Nepal, South Africa, The Philippines, and Vietnam. The Network is under the strategic guidance of the Golden Rice Humanitarian Board and under the management of a network coordinator, based at the International Rice Research Institute (IRRI), in the Philippines. . . .

Biofortified Seeds: A Sustainable Solution

Biofortification—the genetically based complementation for missing micronutrients—of basic staple crops with the help of genetic engineering is presumably the most sustainable and cost-effective approach to reduce micronutrient malnutrition among poor populations in developing countries. Golden Rice is the first example of such an approach. Public sector investment to develop the basic technology has been relatively modest, amounting to about US$2.4 million between 1992 and 2000. To date, Syngenta has invested a similar amount. Product development, however, is time-consuming and requires substantial additional funding. Funds for product development are usually not provided by the public sector or academia, since the type of work that this activity entails normally does not lead to scientific discovery. Costs increase even more dramatically when it comes to biosafety assessment, as required for regulatory approval purposes.

But once a novel, biofortified variety has been approved and handed over to farmers, the system can develop its full potential. From this point on, the technology is built into each and every seed and does not require any additional investments. Consider the potential of a single Golden Rice seed: A single plant produces in the order of 1,000 seeds; within four generations—or less than two years—that one plant will have generated more than [a trillion] seeds, only limited by available land, of course. This would represent up to 28-thousand metric tons of rice, which would be sufficient to feed 100-thousand poor people for one year. And if these people were eating Golden Rice they would be automatically supplemented with provitamin A, thus substantially improving their vitamin A status. This gained protection is cost-free and sustainable. All a farmer needs to benefit from the technology is contained in a seed!

8

Genetic Engineering Is Not a Solution to the Problem of World Hunger

Greenpeace

Greenpeace is an independent campaigning organization that uses nonviolent, creative confrontation to expose global environmental problems and force solutions for a green and peaceful future.

In 2000 a Time *magazine cover proclaimed, "This rice could save a million kids a year." Five years later the promise of Golden Rice, which was supposed to bring an end to vitamin A deficiency (VAD), remains unrealized. Even worse, false claims for Golden Rice are distracting attention and funding from less expensive and more nutritionally sound solutions that really could address the VAD problem.*

Vitamin A is an essential vitamin for humans. It has several functions in the human body and is important for eyesight. Vitamin A deficiency (VAD) can lead to blindness and even death. VAD poses a severe threat to millions of children worldwide, predominantly in the Global South. In 2000, it was reported that rice had been genetically engineered (GE) to contain beta-carotene (pro-vitamin A) in the laboratory. The developers called it "Golden Rice" because the beta-carotene gave it a yellow colour. When the intention to commercialise Golden Rice was announced, it was accompanied

Greenpeace, "All That Glitters Is Not Gold: The False Hope of 'Golden Rice'," *Genetic Engineering Briefing Pack*, May 2005. Reproduced by permission.

by a strident media campaign asserting that Golden Rice could save millions of lives: the headline "This rice could save a million kids a year" appeared on the front page of *Time* magazine [in 2000]. The developer of Golden Rice even placed moral pressure on any organisations or institutions opposed to the cultivation of GE crops: "The consequences will be millions of unnecessary blind children and Vitamin A deficiency related deaths."

In October 2004, [biotech firm] Syngenta announced the harvest of the first ever field trial of Golden Rice in the US, claiming there were "new lines containing significantly higher levels of beta-carotene," although no concentration was given and the full trial results have not been made public.

In April 2005 a new publication by Syngenta presented a new generation of Golden Rice with a twenty-fold higher content of beta-carotene. The GE rice now contains a maximum of 31 micrograms per gram beta-carotene.

Many Questions Remain

This new generation of Golden Rice is far away from actually demonstrating that it has a real potential to alleviate dietary Vitamin A Deficiency (VAD). There are still many factors with this GE rice that have not been addressed: losses of beta-carotene on cooking and storage; availability of other nutrients such as zinc and fat that are necessary to uptake beta carotene into the human body and convert it into Vitamin A (bioavailability).

In the article, the authors simply state: "Definitive statements on the benefit of Golden Rice for the alleviation of vitamin A deficiency cannot be made. The vitamin A delivered and its impact on the body depends on several unquantified factors, including beta-carotene uptake and conversion to vitamin A, as well as the amount of rice consumed by the individual. These factors are under rigorous investigation at present but for the time being only estimates are available."

The rate of absorption of beta-carotene and its conversion to vitamin A is dependent on many factors such as the biochemical quality of the compounds or the occurrence of other components in the diet such as oil and zinc. Because of these factors, the conversion ratio ranges from less than 12:1 up to 2:1. The actual conversion rate for beta-carotene in Golden Rice is still not known. Losses of beta-carotene during cooking have already been reported and losses during storage are expected—both of which can severely undermine the effectiveness of Golden Rice.

Health and Environmental Risks

There are several unexpected effects in Golden Rice, which raise important questions concerning human health safety and nutritional quality. From the GE inserts, Golden Rice originally should have been red (due to the presence of lycopene) but to the surprise of the scientists, it turned out yellow (due to the presence of beta-carotene). The question why the GE rice is yellow and not red has only very recently been explained. In addition, unexpected compounds such as lutein and zeaxanthin were formed in the first generation of Golden Rice. In light of this, any risk assessment of the Golden Rice would have to deal with the possibility of these and any other unexpected compounds, which may lead to anti-nutritional, allergenic or even toxic effects in humans.

There is a real chance to combat [vitamin A deficiency] ... without needing to resort to the high-risk strategy of GE crops.

The environmental risks inherent in GE organisms apply to Golden Rice. Rice is known to cross-pollinate (outcross) and wild and weedy relatives grow in close proximity to rice cultivation. Thus, the spread of genes to conventional and wild varieties of rice is likely to happen over time. This could lead to contamination of wild populations and cultivated seed supply. If a hazardous unexpected effect arises with the GE rice, e.g. increased toxicity or susceptibility to disease, there could be no withdrawal of the gene because of contamination. It is conceivable that this could undermine the food security of a region if the problem became widespread. The case of Golden Rice is a typical example of how little is actually known about the complexity of plant physiology—it would not be surprising if additional unexpected changes in the plant would occur, posing new risks to the environment or human health. Indeed, some unexpected effects in Golden Rice have already been reported. Some of the GE Golden Rice plants of the first generation showed unexplained differences to the respective non-GE control plants: "shorter stature, dark and stay-green nature, and late flowering, and some of them had a much smaller number of seeds."

At present, it is not known what unexpected effects have occurred in the new generation of Golden Rice, but it's clear that the developers still do not have a full understanding of how this GE rice accumulates beta-carotene.

Golden Rice Is Not Necessary

Existing solutions: Options exist to defeat vitamin A deficiency. There are many food sources that contain a naturally high amount of beta-carotene. Examples include refined red palm oil, carrots, leafy green vegetables, sweet potato, cassava, mango, papaya and watermelon.

Existing options to defeat vitamin A deficiencies are detailed in a report, commissioned by Greenpeace: "Vitamin A Deficiency: Diverse Causes, Diverse Solutions." Although VAD is still a problem, aid agencies state that "very significant progress has been made over the last 15 years" with regard to VAD. There is a real chance to combat VAD using existing methods, without needing to resort to the high-risk strategy of GE crops. In general, it is acknowledged that VAD is not a problem lacking in solutions, but the problem is whether VAD is given enough priority by international, regional and national politicians and policy makers.

GE rice is an unnecessary high-tech solution with . . . severe potential to endanger the environment.

Combating VAD requires action at several different levels: on individual/household and on a population level; on daily and on long-term bases; with preventative and with remedial treatment. The factors that contribute to VAD are as diverse as the solutions. There are two basic strategies to reduce VAD: medicine-based strategies and food-based strategies.

Medicine-based strategies include supplementation with vitamin A tablets. The Micronutrient Initiative and UNICEF [United Nations Children's Fund] state that 43 countries now have formal supplementation programmes reaching at least two-thirds of all young children, and that 10 have virtually eliminated VAD.

Food-based strategies include "home gardens," where vegetables are grown in household gardens. The strategy of home gardens is quite promising because an estimated 50% of the undernourished are small scale farmers and only 20% are urban poor who may not have access to a garden. For example, a study in Bangladesh showed that 75g [less than 3 ounces] of Indian Spinach, a low cost green leafy vegetable available all year round in Bangladesh, provides enough pro-vitamin A on a daily basis.

The current successful approaches to combating VAD should be supported on all possible levels. The Golden Rice project does not look to be very promising in this context. GE rice is an unnecessary high-tech solution with too many open questions and severe potential to endanger the environment.

Beta-carotene occurs even naturally in some rice varieties—whole grain rice is a high value component of daily diet, supporting people with starch, protein, minerals and oil. This is not the case with GE rice enriched in one isolated nutrient such as Golden Rice. A number of regional varieties of rice have been identified so far, which naturally contain a certain amount of beta-carotene. Recent findings are about 0.13 [micrograms per gram] in the Philippines with new analyses of up to 0.38 [micrograms per gram]. Unlike Golden Rice, the beta-carotene resides in the outer layers of rice. This means it is lost on milling but the outer layers are also rich in lipids including unsaturated fatty acids, which would aid the bioavailability of beta-carotene. Thus the use of current biodiversity looks much more promising than the use of biotechnology-derived GE rice.

Distracting Attention from Real Solutions

There are many unanswered questions and known problems concerning Golden Rice:

- The conversion ratio of beta-carotene in Golden Rice to vitamin A is not known.

- The complexity of the genetic engineering and the extent to which the metabolic pathways in the plant were changed increase the potential for unexpected and unpredictable effects, thus raising severe concerns concerning human food safety.

- It is known that GE rice can outcross to wild and weedy relatives, raising cultural, agronomic and environmental problems.

The Golden Rice project lacks a coherent idea of how the VAD syndrome could be fought in a convincing and efficient way. The high risks of growing and using GE Golden Rice as food to alleviate vitamin A deficiency is not at all justified by the theoretical benefits. Other approaches to combat vitamin A deficiency, such as home gardening that are successful, effective, and improve nutrition in general are available. Golden Rice is distracting attention and funding from real solutions to tackle VAD.

Not all that glitters is gold!

9

Hunger Should Be Fought at the Local Level

Christine Ahn

Christine Ahn is program coordinator for the Economic and Social Human Rights Program at Food First/Institute for Food and Development Policy.

Throughout the United States, many people do not have access to safe and nutritious food. Many poor neighborhoods do not have supermarkets. Food-borne illnesses occur frequently due to large-scale food processing, and corporate consolidation of the food industry means that just ten companies supply more than half the food and drink sold. A diverse coalition of activists are organizing to achieve food security for local communities, assuring that everyone has a safe, culturally acceptable, nutritious diet, raised through a food system that maximizes self-reliance and social justice.

The U.S. is the world's largest producer and exporter of food, yet in 2002, 35 million Americans didn't know where their next meal was coming from. At the same time, nearly two-thirds of Americans were overweight. Although hunger is still a reality for those living in poverty, our food system has created a condition where "obesity is now a greater threat to the health and well-being of America's poor" than hunger.

Christine Ahn, "Breaking Ground: The Community Food Service Movement," *Backgrounder*, vol. 10, Winter 2004. Copyright © 2004 Food First/Institute for Food and Development Policy. All rights reserved. Reproduced by permission.

A Multifaceted Problem

One reason the food system is so sick is that supermarkets are virtually nonexistent in poor communities. Wealthier neighborhoods have two to three times as many supermarkets as lower-income areas, and white neighborhoods have up to four times more supermarkets than African-American neighborhoods. Without access to nutritious food, poor communities will have unhealthy diets.

Access to safe and nutritious food concerns not only America's poor. Approximately 2,000 Americans die each year from food poisoning caused by salmonella and E. coli, in part due to large-scale food processing. And in our industrialized, profit-maximizing agricultural system, mad cow disease has now become a reality.

Today, just ten companies supply more than half the food and drink sold in the United States. Corporate consolidation of the food industry has reduced farmers to less than 1 percent of the U.S. population, and because production and distribution is so centralized, food now travels on average 1,500 to 2,500 miles from farm to plate in the U.S.

CSAs, also known as subscription farms, allow consumers to buy advance shares of a farm's harvest.

Recognizing that dramatic changes aren't imminent in the profit-driven food system, a diverse network of activists across America have begun organizing for a just food system that benefits consumers and farmers. Family farm groups, food banks, community gardeners, nutritionists, environmentalists, and community development organizations are striving to achieve *community food security* —a condition wherein everyone has a safe, culturally acceptable, nutritious diet through a sustainable food system that maximizes community self-reliance and social justice.

According to Andy Fisher, Executive Director of the Community Food Security Coalition, this movement, which has flowered [since 1997], seeks to democratize food production and distribution by localizing food, using more sustainable and health-promoting practices, and meeting the needs of underserved communities.

Dr. Joan Gussow, Professor Emerita of Nutrition at Columbia University and author of *This Organic Life* (2002), believes that "the Community Food Security movement is still small when compared to the power of . . . Wal-Mart, but all across the country, our growth can almost match theirs."

Innovative Models of Food Justice

Two trends form important pillars of the community food security movement: farmers' markets and community supported agriculture programs (CSAs). Farmers' markets, the most obvious outlets for farmers to earn a decent price for their produce, have grown from 1,774 to 3,100 [since the 1990s]. CSAs, also known as subscription farms, allow consumers to buy advance shares of a farm's harvest. They date back thirty years to Japan, where a group of women concerned about growing food imports, use of pesticides, and the corresponding decrease in the farming population organized a direct relationship with local farms. CSAs have since spread to Europe and to the U.S., where over 1,200 now flourish.

The following are some snapshots of what community food security looks like in the United States.

New York's Just Food

In 2003, 1.6 million people in New York state received emergency food, further stressing the soup kitchens and food pantries that fed 45 percent more people in 2002 than in 2000. And from 1987 to 1997, the state lost about a million acres of fertile farmland, displacing family farmers.

In response to these crises, Just Food began connecting farmers with urban families in the New York City area. Since

1996, Just Food has organized thirty community gardens and thirty-five CSAs, with each CSA supporting up to six regional farmers. During the harvest season, the CSA farmers deliver produce and meat—usually organic and always fresh—to a central distribution site in the city. According to Dr. Gussow, who chairs the Just Food board, demand has soared faster than local farmers can supply.

Food ... is personal and universal to everyone and is fundamental to the inner workings of a community.

Boston's Food Project

Transforming vacant lots into lush city farms is a crucial way to feed a rapidly growing urban population, and the Boston-based Food Project has become a national inspiration to other inner city communities. In 1991, the first growing season yielded 4,000 pounds of food from 2.5 acres of detoxified soil. By 2001, the Food Project was growing 209,000 pounds of organic food on a twenty-one-acre farm and three city lots. The project donates 55 percent of the food to fifteen homeless shelters and soup kitchens, sells 5 percent at reasonable prices at inner city farmers' markets, and distributes the rest to 225 CSA shareholders.

The Food Project also gives youth a chance to learn urban farming, work in Boston homeless shelters, and run city farmers' markets. As youth coordinator Anim Steele puts it, "We need to involve young people because they will inherit our practices, and they need to learn that alternatives exist."

Oakland's Peoples' Grocery

Hamburgers, pizza, Chinese take-out, and donuts are some of the most accessible foods for West Oakland, California's 30,000 predominantly African American and Latino residents. This impoverished neighborhood has just one grocery store, forty liquor stores, and a handful of fast food restaurants.

In response, community activists started Peoples' Grocery, a community garden and mobile market in the heart of West Oakland. They transformed a 4,000 square foot vacant lot into a garden that now grows seasonal fruits and vegetables and educates youth and residents about urban renewal, food justice, and revitalizing the local economy. They also operate a mobile market on wheels that runs on bio-diesel fuel and sells fresh produce, staple goods, and healthy snacks from local farmers and urban farmers' markets.

According to co-founder Brahm Ahmadi, Peoples' Grocery was founded "with the long-term goal of building community self-reliance in West Oakland. We've chosen food as an organizing tool for our work because it is personal and universal to everyone and is fundamental to the inner workings of a community."

Junk food or Just Food? Feeding Our Children

As Ahmadi says, the community food security movement is about organizing, and the community doesn't stop at the school gates.

Nationwide, a coalition of students, parents, teachers, administrators, and community and health advocates are pressing for farm-to-school programs that help local farmers supply schools with nutritious food. In 1997, the Santa Monica–Malibu Unified School District became the first to stock fresh produce from a farmers' market in the salad bars of all its nine schools. Over 700 school districts across America now participate in farm-to-school programs, and the trend is spreading to universities and other public institutions, including the Connecticut Department of Corrections.

Since 1999, the Berkeley Unified School District has purchased from local farmers to feed its 10,000 students. Berkeley also serves fresh food in its cafeterias through school gardens, such as the Martin Luther King Jr. Middle School's Edible Schoolyard, founded by Chez Panisse chef Alice Waters.

In Los Angeles, the organizing efforts of students, parents, and teachers resulted in a ban on sales of soda and junk food in cafeterias and student stores throughout the school district. Other districts are considering such a ban.

This organizing is in response to an estimate that one-third of our nation's 23,000 public schools sell fast food to students, often because tight food budgets lead administrators to resort to cheap, highly processed food. In Los Angeles—which serves fast food to its students—75 percent of students participate in the USDA's [U.S. Department of Agriculture's] National School Lunch Program, which reimburses L.A. schools approximately $33 million per year, thereby subsidizing the sale of fast food to children. Since school breakfast and lunch are often the only meals low income children get all day, the impact on the health of poor students is potentially disastrous. As fifteen-year-old Rosa Villar, a Los Angeles high school student, put it, "If schools are responsible for teaching kids to say no to drugs, tobacco, and alcohol, then why don't they tell kids to say no to fast food?"

Clearly, change is needed on a large scale, including at the level of the National School Lunch Program. Groups within the movement have successfully pressed for national legislation, such as the Community Food Security Act of the 1996 Farm Bill, authorizing $16 million in USDA-funded grants over seven years to support projects that provide fresher, more nutritious food in poor neighborhoods and help communities meet their own food needs. Advocates succeeded in doubling this amount in the 2002 Farm Bill. They are now pressing for federal funds to assist schools with the extra costs of purchasing directly from local farmers and for transit programs and distribution centers to improve food access in both urban and rural low income communities.

The Way Forward

Organizing around food is often a catalyst for addressing broader social and economic justice issues, such as access to affordable housing and public transportation. The proliferation of local food projects, farmers' markets, CSAs, farm-to-school programs, and progressive public policies aimed at both supplying wholesome food to all and stemming the loss of family farms should restore hope that, as Andy Fisher says, "another food system is possible."

These stories do not just describe isolated pockets of change. The fusing of the community food security and justice movement with the movement challenging globalization and corporate hegemony could spell the beginning of the end of the industrial food system.

10

Women Are Key to Solving the Hunger Problem

Katharine Coon

Katharine Coon is a nutritionist for the Nutrition and Gender Initiative for the International Center for Research on Women, based in Washington, D.C.

Throughout the developing world, women have the primary responsibility for providing food, fuel, water and child care for their families. The best way to reduce hunger is to address discrimination faced by women in the areas of access to education and resources.

Women throughout the developing world bear primary responsibility for the procurement and preparation of food, fuel and water for their households as well as caring for their children's health, education and overall well-being. At the same time, the discrimination faced by women in access to education and productive resources, combined with the restrictive violence many face in their homes and communities, undermines their ability to provide adequate food and care for their children. In this way, gender discrimination itself is a fundamental cause of hunger and malnutrition, especially among children.

Mounting Evidence

Our current understanding of the importance of women's status and access to resources in combating malnutrition and disease throughout the lifecycle is based on evidence dating to the 1990s, when researchers began documenting differential impacts of income controlled by women versus men on household consumption patterns. The data showed that higher shares of household income controlled by women are associated with higher expenditures on children and reductions in the prevalence of child malnutrition.

A separate study of data sets from 36 developing countries in Asia, Latin America and sub-Saharan Africa show that improvements in women's status—defined as their decision-making power relative to men in their households and communities—is significantly associated with reduced child malnutrition rates.

Another analysis found that improvements in women's education, which is closely associated with control over income and status, was twice as powerful as increased food availability in explaining reductions in children's malnutrition rates between 1970 and 1995 in 63 countries.

Women and girls need access to education, land, credit, ... new productive technologies, ... and training.

Moreover, a qualitative study in Nigeria found children's nutritional status was significantly better in female-headed households than in male-headed ones with the same or higher incomes. And a second generation of similar studies, using increasingly sophisticated analytic techniques, are confirming these findings and extending them to analyses of household health expenditures.

Challenges for policy and program development

Despite the mounting evidence that improving women's education, income and status helps break the hunger-malnutrition-poverty cycle, women and girls throughout the developing world continue to face discrimination and violence in their homes and communities.

Women and girls need access to education, land, credit, complementary inputs, new productive technologies, extension services and training. Increasingly, researchers, activists and development organizations across all sectors are acknowledging these needs through strong pro-active policies to increase girls' access to education, promote women's presence and voice in decision-making bodies at all levels of society, and guarantee and increase women's access to productive resources.

But to fully succeed, all community members need to be engaged in processes which help raise their awareness and understanding of how discriminatory gender norms undermine their communities' social and economic development. Case studies of 16 projects in Niger, Kenya, Zambia, and Ghana suggest that raising gender awareness leads to "greater agricultural yield, improved sanitation, improved health and nutrition, and expanded primary school enrollment, especially for girls . . . as men move from initial resistance to active support . . . and divide household and farm work more equitably."

A Simple but Powerful Approach

Whether addressing international development concerns from the perspective of microcredit, water and sanitation, health, or agricultural production and marketing, programs which also increase gender equity within households and communities see an additional payoff in terms of reduced malnutrition. If these efforts seek to improve both gender equity and nutrition, then the payoff is even greater.

In Ghana, for example, women's micro-credit loan institutions have found they can reduce rates of sickness and malnutrition among children by providing members with ongoing nutrition education classes. Working in five sites in Africa, Latin America, and Asia, ICRW [International Center for Research on Women] enabled women to improve their families' nutrition by providing them with extension resources, nutrition education, and opportunities to participate in active decision-making. The Agriculture-Nutrition Advantage project sought to reduce hunger in four African countries by educating key technical specialists and country leaders on the benefits of linking gender, nutrition, and agriculture.

The basic thrust of the approach being described is simple but powerful: by linking gender and nutrition to projects in a variety of traditionally isolated development "sectors," the payoff in development investments to reduce poverty, hunger, and malnutrition is greater than would be achieved from investing in any single component alone.

11

Small Farms Are Key to Solving the Hunger Problem

Julie Mardin

Julie Mardin is a freelance writer and photographer as well as a past board member and regular contributor to the Light Millennium Web site.

The success of small family farms is key to solving the problem of world hunger. Yet many such farmers find themselves working in a hostile environment, burdened with expensive technologies that have robbed them of the ancient wisdom that comes from living close to the land. Free-trade agreements such as the North American Free Trade Agreement (NAFTA) have caused payments to farmers to fall while costs to consumers have risen, and corporate agriculture has forced many small farmers out of business. If hunger is to be alleviated, conditions must be created that allow small farmers to prosper.

At the last WTO [World Trade Organization] conference in Cancun, Mexico, South Korean farmer Lee Kyung Hae, wearing a placard that said, WTO KILLS FARMERS, climbed a police barricade, and plunged a small Swiss Army knife into his heart.

Back in his home in the mountain slopes south of Seoul, Lee had created Seoul Farm, 30 hectares [74 acres] of grazing pastures, paddy fields and buildings, housing and sheds miraculously built on steeply wooded slopes. Nobody could have imagined cows grazing at such a gradient, or conceived of the mini cable-car to transport hay from the higher slopes to sheds below. His farm became a teaching college with live-in students, and his fame had grown as a visionary farm leader who had mastered a hostile land. In 1988 he had won a UN [United Nations] award for rural leadership.

Yet after agricultural reforms put in motion by the Uruguay Round (which later became the WTO), South Korea started to reduce agricultural subsidies and opened its markets to highly subsidized food imports, leading to a collapse in the price of beef, and the eventual foreclosure of the Seoul Farm. Lee became an active fighter against the policies of the WTO, going on hunger strike thirty times. Even though he entered politics, and was elected to his state legislature three times as a farmer representative, none of these paths seemed to be sufficient for him to effect change and help protect farmers from free trade.

Globalization Has Hurt Small Farmers

As Lee's regretful sacrifice alarmingly alerts us, one of the casualties of globalization has been the small family farmer, sadly in more than just metaphorical terms. In fact, the suicide rate among farmers worldwide is far higher than among the regular population. In England and Canada it is twice the national average. In India, there appears to be a virtual epidemic. Nearly 2,000 farmers have committed suicide in [the Indian state of] Rajasthan [in the years 2001–2004]. In the cotton growing areas of India, more than 10,000 farmers are said to have committed suicide over the past 20 years, many of them by drinking the pesticides that failed them.

When one comes to think of the technology that was sold to these farmers, one can see it as a sort of trap. It is true, Indian farmers were jubilant in the early 1980s when the fourth generation pesticides synthetic pyrethoids were introduced in the cotton growing areas of the country. For the first two or three years, the chemical killed almost everything in sight, the targeted pest, the "American bollworm," as well as all the beneficial insects. Slowly, however, the bollworms developed resistance to the sprays, the number of costly and toxic sprays increased, as did the resistance to the chemicals. Along with crop failures came mounting debt. I am not even getting into the environmental hazards of such substances in terms of the physical well-being of the farmer, the land, and the consumer, but purely the economic ones.

Those who look for technology to answer the world's hunger problems are missing part of the picture.

Those same people who promoted the Green Revolution technology, often do generously acknowledge the environmental hazards of their past methods, especially when they are promoting their new "green" solution, which is bio-engineered crops, such as Bt cotton, incorporating a gene from a soil-borne bacterium, *Bacillus thuringiensis* (Bt), and, so they say, precluding the need for any pesticides. Bt cotton is touted as a success story in China, but what is not as widely discussed is the fact that they have started having to spray pesticides in order to deal with the third and fourth generation of the American bollworm insects, due to a growing resistance to the Bt gene. It is widely accepted that the third generation of the pest presents the most challenge. Scientists are now trying to create new genetically manipulated varieties with two Bt genes. What next? asks trade policy analyst, Devinder Sharma. The gene from a scorpion, or a snake? It seems the farmer will now be faced with a far more dangerous and untested biological treadmill, as well as the chemical one, that has created an ongoing cycle of poison.

Local Solutions Lead to Higher Productivity

Those who look for technology to answer the world's hunger problems are missing part of the picture. In terms of regaining the health and productivity of the land, we have to, to a certain extent, undo the elaborate mechanisms that we have painstakingly built up over the past decades, stop burdening farmers with these unsustainable and expensive techniques, and return to some of the old wisdom. There are a few examples we can look at. For instance, Indonesia in the mid 1980s, when President Suharto faced a crisis with brown plant hopper insects and their devastated rice crops. He decided to heed controversial advice from the FAO [Food and Agriculture Organization] at the UN and the International Rice Institute, to ban 57 pesticides and institute a nation-wide integrated pest management program. Despite dire warnings from the chemical industry, led by the American Embassy in Jakarta, that Indonesia would be risking an epidemic of hunger and starvation, in the next two years, rice production increased by 18%, pesticide consumption was drastically reduced, as was the cost of cultivation.

Similarly, with the collapse of the Soviet Union, and the loss of its cheap oil supply, Cuba had to undergo a major rethinking of its methods of supplying food for its population. As the value of their foreign exchange also dropped, they were unable to obtain the same amount of food imports, fertilizers and pesticides, which had something like an 80% drop in availability. They had to return to a largely organic farming technology, involving biological substitutes for the chemical fertilizers, such as composts, earthworks, green manure, and instead of pesticides using integrated pest management techniques, planting resistant plants, rotating crops, and using microbial agents to combat plant pathogens. They also carried out a major program of land reform, where huge inefficient, state-run farms were divided up into smaller co-ops. By 1996, Cuba recorded its highest-ever production levels for 10 of 13 of its basic food items. Productivity increases came primarily from the small farms. The government also threw its support behind a growing urban gardening movement, which has also been extremely important to the recovery of the Cuban food supply.

The introduction of new technology has only exacerbated the disparity between the wealthy and poor.

Brazil's fourth largest city, Belo Horizonte, has instigated similar innovations in its urban resources, making city plots available for local, organic farmers, as long as they keep prices within reach of the poor. They have started posting where to find the cheapest prices for over forty food staples, and enhanced nutrition by replacing processed foods with local organic food in school lunches. There is even a campaign to protect those newly arrived from the countryside against global corporate food advertising and the allure of processed foods. What an effect such policies might have in urban centers all over the world, including in first-world cities, with [their] growing problems of homelessness, hunger, as well as the growing epidemic of first-world food diseases, such as diabetes, heart disease and obesity.

And in Kenya, where experts declared the land beyond hope, women of the Green Belt Movement have launched an anti-desertification campaign that has planted 20 million trees, and is beginning to recover diverse, traditional food crops.

Technological Solutions Worsen Matters

While these working solutions may not sound as glamorous and futuristic as others, they represent some of the many citizen-driven projects that are flying in the face of conventional wisdom. For those who claim they are interested in efficiency, just contrast the simplicity of these ideas with the expense in research and development, not to mention public relations, for such risky and untested ventures as bioengineered foods. Think of the new "Golden Rice," that is said to be the answer to preventing blindness in malnourished children in India and other parts of Asia. One analysis calculated that one adult male would have to eat 18 lbs. of the stuff in order to meet his RDA [recommended dietary allowance (of Vitamin A)]. This is not taking into account the amounts of fat and protein also required in order to convert beta carotene into vitamin A, also generally lacking in the diets of the malnourished.

Even if genetically engineered crops were a scientific breakthrough, historically, as post–World War II experiments in "Green Revolution" technology have shown, the introduction of new technology has only exacerbated the disparity between the wealthy and poor, favoring the larger farmers and squeezing out the smaller ones, and increasing the dependence of all on the corporate suppliers. With the movement towards patenting seeds and technology, this lack of control over one's own destiny will be even more intensified.

If we are to alleviate world hunger, we have to create the situation where the small family farmer can prosper again.

Other aspects that have rigged the game against the small producers are free trade agreements, such as NAFTA, which as reported by Food First, have increased rural poverty and inequality, in both the first and the third world, threatened small family farmers, and hurt consumers. The forces that somehow allow the prices that small farmers receive to fall, while consumer prices continue to rise, have only been strengthened.

In the third world, free trade is also often accompanied by structural adjustment policies, imposed by the World Bank and the IMF [International Monetary Fund] as terms of their loans, which means cutbacks in government spending on health, education, and social support. Stable agricultural pricing policies are abandoned in favor of the market, while at the same time first-world countries increase their subsidies to industrial farmers, thus creating a highly unequal trading relationship. State-run industries and utilities are sold off, often at bargain-basement prices, price controls are removed, leading to rapid price increases for basic goods and services, farmland is converted to cash crops for export, rather than food for local communities, making farmers' livelihoods dependent on the vagaries of the international commodities market. These policies have a pretty dismal record in practically every country they have been implemented [in]. Most, instead of increasing prosperity, have again increased the disparity of income, and, contrary to claims, effected a slowdown in economic growth. China, cited once again as the great success story in alleviating its hunger problems, is perhaps unusual as it has so far resisted many of the neo-liberal free market policies imposed by the IMF.

Small Farmers Are Key to Strong Economies

Some might say these are the most efficient systems, [and that] maybe the small family farmer is a thing of the past. In fact, this is the purported philosophy of much of the structural adjustment policies of the World Bank and International Monetary Fund and such philanthropic institutions as the Rockefeller Foundation. Their aim is to convert small farmers' plots into growing cash crops for export, so they can generate enough money to buy cheap first-world imports, and transition into jobs outside of the agricultural sector. And yet such policies have not succeeded in generating the needed employment for displaced farmers, and poverty rates, instability and hunger have only gone up. The most practical and humane tactic seems to be to acknowledge the small family farmer as the basis of local economies and of national economic development. They are in fact, by their history, and through their longer and closer ties, the natural stewards and guardians of the land, insurers of biodiversity, and food security, and in fact what helped today's industrial economic powerhouses like the US, Japan, China, and South Korea get off the ground. People such as Lee Kyung Hae are the building blocks of a strong economy, and a healthy population. It seems if we are to alleviate world hunger, we have to create the situation where the small family farmer can prosper again.

Fair trade allows small farmers to receive fair prices for their products.

One first step towards this goal would be to get rid of first-world export subsidies that do nothing but enhance the exporting power of agribusiness, and that keep third-world markets out of reach of their own local farmers. The yearly subsidy the US gives to its cotton farmers alone is three times our total aid to Africa. Poor nations don't need our aid so much as access to our markets, and especially access to their own. One Food First press release cites $50 billion as the amount third-world nations lose because of US agriculture subsidies, ironically the same amount that the rich nations give in aid to poor countries. While we as tax payers pay for these subsidies that benefit large industrial farmers, we also pay for foreign aid packages that barely make a difference. We have to allow countries to get on their feet by giving them a fair chance at trade, also by giving them back their sovereignty and ability to make their own decisions on tariffs, guarding against dumping, and protecting of local industries, which the industrialized countries have never given up.

If world trade organizations and world trade agreements are to be of any help, they must work to help prevent monopolies, rather than to facilitate them. In order to prevent what threatens to be a corporate takeover of our methods of growing and providing food world wide, we have to give room for local solutions to grow. Also, burdensome and expensive technology needs to be re-evaluated and perhaps discontinued on a state-wide level, to relieve the growing financial burden on farmers keeping up with methods that in the long run seem like they will be unviable anyway. Perhaps governments will begin to see the long term economic sense in having strong environmental laws. In order to achieve this, of course, environmental rules and regulations need to be strengthened, not weakened, by trade agreements. We also have to think locally in terms of our own needs as well. For now, perhaps some of the things individual consumers can do are once again simple: patronize farmers' markets, buy organically grown food whenever you can, not only for your own kitchen, but out at restaurants as well, and support the "fair trade" movement, by buying fair trade products. These are products which have been certified by an independent certification process—Fair Trade Labeling Organizations International—as having been produced without labor abuses and with prices that are higher because of their quality or because they are organic. Fair trade allows small farmers to receive fair prices for their products, and for them to function outside of the system that is so skewed against them.

Organizations to Contact

Agricultural and Food Policy Center (AFPC)
Department of Agricultural Economics
College Station, TX   77843-2124
(979) 845-5913 • fax: (979) 845-3140
e-mail: info@afpc.tamu.edu
Web site: www.afpc.tamu.edu

Texas A & M University's AFPC analyzes the effects of government policy proposals on farmers, businesses, taxpayers, and consumers. It publishes its findings and conducts educational programs.

America's Second Harvest
35 E. Wacker Dr., #2000, Chicago, IL   60601
(800) 771-2303
Web site: www.secondharvest.org

America's Second Harvest is a network of charitable organizations, food banks, and food-rescue organizations. It provides food assistance, publishes resources on hunger in the United States, presents educational programs, and lobbies for public policies that address hunger.

Bread for the World & Bread for the World Institute (BFW)
50 F St. NW, Suite 500, Washington, DC   20001
(202) 639-9400 • fax: (202) 639-9401
Web site: www.bread.org

The BFW is a Christian organization devoted to eliminating hunger and poverty. It conducts research and education on hunger and development and engages in lobbying to seek justice for people affected by poverty and hunger. The BFW Web site provides information on hunger in the United States and throughout the world, including the *Hunger Report, 2006*, which can be downloaded.

Center on Hunger and Poverty
Institute on Assets and Social Policy
Waltham, MA   02454-9110
(781) 736-8885 • fax: (781) 736-3925
email: hunger@brandeis.edu
Web site: www.centeronhunger.org

The Center on Hunger and Poverty conducts research on domestic hunger, child nutrition, and public policy at the local, state, and national levels. It seeks to be a national clearinghouse for information on hunger and food-insecurity issues and works with policy makers and the media to promote understanding of factors impacting hunger in the United States.

Food and Agriculture Organization of the United Nations (FAO)
Viale delle Terme di Caracalla, Rome   00100
  Italy
telephone: (+39) 06 57051 • fax: (+39) 06 570 53152
e-mail: FAO-HQ@fao.org
Web site: www.fao.org

The FAO seeks to serve both developed and developing countries by providing an international forum for policy debate and negotiation in order to build "a world without hunger." The FAO Web site includes a world hunger map and materials on agriculture, biotechnology, biosecurity, nutrition, fisheries, and sustainable development.

International Food Policy Research Institute (IFPRI)
2033 K St. NW, Washington, DC   20006-1002
(202) 862-5600 • fax: (202) 467-4439
e-mail: ifpri@cgiar.org
Web site: www.ifpri.org

IFPRI is a human rights organization that conducts research, formulates policy solutions, and publishes educational materials aimed at building food security and eliminating hunger and malnutrition. *Understanding the Links Between Agriculture and Health* is a May 2006 policy brief published on the IFPRI Web site. It addresses issues such as technology, disease, biodiversity, and climate change as they affect both health and agriculture.

National Center for Food and Agricultural Policy
1616 P St. NW, 1st Fl., Washington, DC   20036
(202) 328-5048 • fax: (202) 328-5133
e-mail: ncfap@ncfap.org
Web site: www.ncfap.org

The National Center for Food and Agricultural Policy conducts research, analysis, and education to inform public policy on food, agriculture, natural resources, environmental quality, and rural economics.

Pew Initiative on Food and Biotechnology
1331 H St. NW, Suite 900, Washington, DC   20005
(202) 347-9044 • fax: (202) 347-9047
Web site: http://pewagbiotech.org

The Pew Initiative on Food and Biotechnology was established in 2001 to be an independent and objective source of credible information on agricultural biotechnology for the public, media, and policy makers. The initiative seeks to provide information and encourage debate and dialogue so that consumers and policy makers can make informed decisions.

Resources for the Future
1616 P St. NW, Washington, DC   20036
(202) 328-5000 • fax: (202) 939-3460
Web site: www.rff.org

Resources for the Future is a nonprofit and nonpartisan organization that conducts independent research—rooted primarily in economics and other social sciences—on international environmental, energy, and natural resource issues.

Rural Development Institute (RDI)
1411 Fourth Ave. Suite 910, Seattle, WA   98101
(206) 528-5880 • fax: (206) 528-5881
email: info@rdiland.org
Web site: www.rdiland.org

The Rural Development Institute is a nonprofit organization that provides legal assistance to the rural poor. The RDI uses farm-level field research and comparative research from around the world to help design and then implement legal and policy measures that support peaceful, democratic approaches to land reform.

Share Our Strength (SOS)
1730 M St. NW, Suite 700, Washington, DC   20036
(800) 969-4767
email: info@strength.org
Web site: www.strength.org

Share our Strength is a private nonprofit organization that supports efforts to address the root causes of hunger and poverty. It awards grants to support nonprofit organizations that provide food assistance and nutrition education. SOS builds coalitions between volunteers, culinary professionals, and businesses such as restaurants and food cooperatives to address the problem of world hunger in a variety of national and international contexts.

World Hunger Education Service
PO Box 29056, Washington, DC   20017
(202) 269-6322
e-mail: hungernotes@aol.com
Web site: www.worldhunger.org

The World Hunger Education Service is a nonprofit organization that does research and publishes information on the world hunger problem. It views hunger in the context of international economics and works to obtain a just economic order.

World Hunger Year (WHY)
505 Eighth Ave., Suite 2100, New York, NY   10018-6582
(212) 629-8850 • fax: (212) 465-9274
Web site: www.worldhungeryear.org

WHY is a not-for-profit organization founded by talk-show host Bill Ayres and the late singer-songwriter Harry Chapin. WHY supports community-based organizations that build self-sufficiency by offering job training, education, and after-school programs; increasing access to housing and health care; and providing microcredit and entrepreneurial opportunities.

Worldwatch Institute
1776 Massachusetts Ave. NW, Washington, DC   20036-1904
(202) 452-1999 • fax: (202) 296-7365
e-mail: worldwatch@worldwatch.org
Web site: www.worldwatch.org

The Worldwatch Institute is an independent, interdisciplinary research organization that works to inform policy makers and the public about global and environmental issues. It seeks to be "a leading source of information on the interactions among key environmental, social, and economic trends." Among its many publications are *State of the World*, an annual report on global environmental issues; and *World Watch Magazine*, which addresses issues including population, climate change, human behavior, and social policy.

Bibliography

Books

Romeo Bertolini — *Making Information and Communication Technologies Work for Food Security in Africa.* Washington, DC: International Food Policy Research Institute, 2004.

Bread for the World Institute — *Are We on Track to End Hunger? Hunger Report 2004: 14th Annual Report on the State of World Hunger.* Washington, DC: Bread for the World Institute, 2004.

Christopher Cook — *Diet for a Dead Planet: How the Food Industry Is Killing Us.* New York: New Press, 2004.

Carole Counihan — *Food in the USA: A Reader.* New York: Routledge, 2002.

Jenny Edkins — *Whose Hunger? Concepts of Famine, Practices of Aid.* Minneapolis: University of Minnesota Press, 2002.

Ana Gonzalez-Pelaez — *Human Rights and World Trade: Hunger in International Society.* New York: Routledge, 2005.

Peter Griffiths — *The Economist's Tale: A Consultant Encounters Hunger and the World Bank.* New York: Zed, 2003.

Suraiya Jabeen Ismail et al. — *Community-Based Food and Nutrition Programmes: What Makes Them Successful.* Rome: Food and Agriculture Organization of the United Nations, 2003.

Bjorn Lomborg — *Global Crises, Global Solutions.* New York: Cambridge University Press. 2004.

George S. McGovern — *The Third Freedom: Ending Hunger in Our Time.* Lanham, MD: Rowman & Littlefield, 2002.

George McGovern, Bob Dole, and Donald E. Messer — *Ending Hunger Now: A Challenge to Persons of Faith.* Minneapolis: Fortress, 2005.

Per Pinstrup-Andersen and Ebbe Schioler — *Seeds of Contention: World Hunger and the Global Controversy over GM Crops.* Oxford: Oxford University Press, 2003.

Thomas W. Pogge — *World Poverty and Human Rights: Cosmopolitan Responsibilities and Reforms.* Malden, MA: Polity, 2005.

George Pyle   *Raising Less Corn, More Hell: The Case for the Independent Farm and Against Industrial Food.* New York: Public Affairs, 2005.

C. Ford Runge   *Ending Hunger in Our Lifetime: Food Security and Globalization.* Baltimore: Johns Hopkins University Press, 2003.

Sharman Apt Russell   *Hunger: An Unnatural History.* New York: Basic Books, 2005.

Pedro A. Sanchez   *Halving Hunger: It Can Be Done.* Sterling, VA: Earthscan, 2005.

Loretta Schwartz-Nobel   *Growing Up Empty: The Hunger Epidemic in America.* New York: HarperCollins, 2002.

Monkombu Sambasivan Swaminathan, Pedro Medrano, and R.V. Bhavani   *Towards a Hunger-Free World: The Ethical Dimensions.* Madras, India: East West, 2004.

Brian Tokar   *Gene Traders: Biotechnology, World Trade, and the Globalization of Hunger.* Burlington, VT: Toward Freedom, 2004.

| R.C. Verma | *Terror by Hunger*. New Delhi: Aravali, 2003. |

Periodicals

Clifton E. Anderson	"Biotech on the Farm: Realizing the Promise," *Futurist*, September/October 2005.
David Bennett	"World Hunger Report Shows Number of Malnourished Rising," *Southwest Farm Press*, January 22, 2004.
Christian Science Monitor	"World Hunger: The Solution Starts with Respect," December 5, 2005.
Kevin Clarke	"Heed the Hungry: Forcing Genetically Modified Food on Unwilling People Makes Us Corporal Dorks of Mercy," *U.S. Catholic*, January 2003.
Nafi Diouf	"Starving Children Hope, Wait," *Seattle Times*, July 25, 2005.
Robert F. Drinan	"Report Shows World Hunger Increasing," *National Catholic Reporter*, April 2, 2004.
Ecologist	"Engineering Hunger," May 2003.

Food Engineering   "Process Food: Reduce World Hunger," January 2004.

Carmen G. Gonzalez   "Trade Liberalization, Food Security, and the Environment: The Neo-Liberal Threat to Sustainable Rural Development," *Transnational Law and Contemporary Problems*, Fall 2004.

Bryan Hall and J. Larry Brown   "Food Security Among Older Adults in the United States," *Topics in Clinical Nutrition*, October/December 2005.

Brian Halweil   "The Irony of Climate: Archaeologists Suspect That a Shift in the Planet's Climate Thousands of Years Ago Gave Birth to Agriculture. Now Climate Change Could Spell the End of Farming as We Know It," *World Watch*, March/April 2005.

Carl F. Jordan   "Genetic Engineering, The Farm Crisis and World Hunger," *BioScience*, June 2002.

Donald Kennedy   "Agriculture and the Developing World," *Science*, October 17, 2003.

Lancet   "Boosting the Effectiveness of Food Aid," October 22, 2005.

Trudy Lieberman — "Hungry in America," *Nation*, August 18, 2003.

Amy MacLachlan — "The Hidden Hunger: Ending Micronutrient Malnutrition a Worthwhile Challenge," *Presbyterian Record*, December 2004.

Suzanne McCabe — "World Hunger: A Global Problem," *Junior Scholastic*, March 8, 2004.

Michael McCarthy — "UN Backs GM Crops Despite Concerns That Benefits Do Not Reach the World's Poor," *Independent* (London), May 18, 2004.

Clare McKeever — "'I Am Working and Hungry,'" *Sojourners*, June 2005.

Minneapolis Star Tribune — "Q & A George McGovern: Maybe for the First Time in Human History We Can Resolve World Hunger," November 21, 2004.

Shaena Montanari — "Global Climate Change Linked to Increasing World Hunger," *World Watch*, September/October 2005.

Timothy F. Murphy and Gladys B. White "Dead Sperm Donors or World Hunger: Are Bioethicists Studying the Right Stuff?" *Hastings Center Report*, March/April 2005.

Saint Louis Post-Dispatch "Anti-Poverty Group Calls Modified Crops Helpful; 222 Million Acres Were Planted Around the World Last Year," January 12, 2006.

Sally Schuff "Hunger Relief Simply Not a Topic for Trade Negotiators," *Feedstuffs*, August 2, 2004.

Seattle Times "2005 a Banner Year for GM Crops, Engineered Food: Activists Claim Little Being Done to End World Hunger," January 12, 2006.

Clare Ulrich "Enlightened Policies Can Benefit Poor and Hungry," *Human Ecology*, August 2005.

Index